THE
APPLE
CONNECTION

APPLE COOKERY

with flavor, fact and folklore,
from memories, libraries and kitchens
of old and new friends – and strangers

compiled at
cranberrie cottage in
granville centre, nova scotia, by

Beatrice Ross Buszek

The recipes in this book
were hand-lettered by
Beatrice Ross Buszek
at Cranberrie Cottage
in Nova Scotia, Canada

Published by Nimbus Publishing Limited
P.O. Box 9301, Station A
Halifax, Nova Scotia
B3K 5N5

ISBN 0-920852-48-3

First printing 1985
Second printing 1985
Third printing 1987
Fourth printing 1988
Fifth printing 1990

Printed and bound in Canada by Wm. MacNab & Son Ltd., Halifax, Nova Scotia

Distributed in the United States by Yankee Books, Camden, Maine, 04843

A DEDICATION...
With love,
to my grandchildren,
Kristin, Nathan and Brian,
and Thomas Joseph.

ACKNOWLEDGEMENT

After eight years of kitchen, library and attic research, it is not possible to adequately acknowledge the many people whose ideas led to other ideas, whose favourite recipes were shared, whose support or criticism influenced each of the five **Connections**.

The Apple Connection benefited from the literature and the tested recipes from government departments across Canada and the United States. To the six friends who assisted in testing some of the other concoctions, and to their families who endorsed or rejected them, I owe special thanks. Grateful acknowledgement is given to the many food editors and radio and television personnel who provided generous and enthusiastic interviews and commentary.

My daughter, Christine, did the sketches in **The Apple Connection** and designed the cover. I am, as always, uniquely indebted to her.

Sincere appreciation to John Garrison and his staff at MacNab Printers in Halifax who have, for the past six years, stood by me and protected the quality of the books. A year ago Nimbus Publishing Limited in Halifax took over as publisher. It has been difficult to relinquish the parental role and I acknowledge here the enormous patience and understanding of the Editor and other staff who are committed to keep intact the Cranberrie flavour and format of the five **Connections**. It is good to be associated with this fine Maritime publishing company.

To all those not mentioned here who have come to my assistance, knowingly or otherwise, sincere acknowledgement is given.

APPLES...

Entrees
with meat and fish

Entrees
with vegetables

Stuffings

Salads

Soups

Desserts

Cakes and Cookies

Drinks

A is for

Pies

INTRODUCTION

The apple is the fruit of the Annapolis Valley. Years of apple harvest have identified the fertile valley, where Cranberrie Cottage stands, with some of the world's best orchards. Therefore it seemed quite appropriate to complete the Cranberrie Cottage culinary capers with **The Apple Connection**.

In much the same way as those that preceded it, the apple book soon became more than a foray of orchards and libraries and experiments in the kitchen. In the midst of the research, old memories were alerted and my mind raced back fifty years, sorting out and retrieving bits and parts of my apple heritage. Long forgotten events, important at the time, were brought back to life.

At the Legislative Library in Halifax, in several large, green, bound volumes, in poetry, prose and pictures, is the history of the famous Nova Scotia Apple Blossom Festivals. Those were the hey-day years of apple production in the province, and the festivals, held annually in the town of Kentville, paid local homage and "internationally publicized the beauty of the orchards of Nova Scotia in bloom." As I leafed through the books and lingered on the old pictures, I smiled, thinking, not of the first but of the third festival in 1935 when I was twelve years old.

The depression barely touched the lives of rural Nova Scotians because for them life had always been hard and money and jobs scarce. I was a child of those years and my world centered around the church and the community of a country village. It was no small happening when our two-room school was selected, from all the rural schools in the county, to participate in the next Apple Blossom celebration.

Each year the festival had a different theme. For 1935 someone envisioned hundreds of multicoloured Maypole dances, a seemingly chaste and decorous rite to honour the miracle of the blossoms. On the fated day, hundreds of school children skipped and tripped onto the field to the shrill notes of the swirling skirted pipers. And then, having practiced to perfection, we picked up the long ribbons and wove them in and out and under to make a perfect Maypole. All the girls wore new white sneakers and coloured cotton dresses and sang with all their might, "Come Lasses and Lads, Take leave of your dads, And away to the Maypole — *Heigh*!". I was as close to heaven that day as I ever expected to be.

Such enthusiasm would seem absurd now, but back in 1935 the twenty miles to Kentville was a journey, and for most of us it was the first train ride, and a new pair of white sneakers at the end of May was an unheard of luxury. They cost ninety-five cents and one girl could not afford them and had to withdraw. Another girl said she bought her dress at Stedmans for a dollar. After weeks of fanciful deliberation, the great decision was made and mother ordered my first store-bought dress from Eaton's catalogue.

As the train approached Grand Pré and Wolfville, there were miles of orchards as far as the eye could see, bedecked in deep pink buds about to bloom. The early June air, though cool, was saturated with the heady pervasive bouquet of apple orchards in the spring. In the distance, across the dykes and red waters of Minas Basin loomed the legendary Cape Blomidon. The school term really ended that day although we attended classes until the end of the month. Most of that time we daydreamed, reliving those moments when, for a little while, we were removed from our everyday lives.

In my village almost everybody had at least two apple trees but there were' few large orchards. Every fall father put a barrel of Northern Spys and a barrel of Winter Gravensteins and a box of Russets in the basement. Apples were accepted as if they went naturally with a house and land in much the same way as old lilacs and roses. I can remember thinking that God made apples just to make apple pie, probably because my mother made the best apple pie in the world. It is no wonder that father would top off breakfast with cold, deep, nutmeg-flavoured, tart apple pie and that I caught the habit. Now my children and grandchildren love apple pie in the morning, but I've never been able to surpass the ones Mother made when I was twelve years old.

In the thirty years before I returned to Nova Scotia, I was fortunate to live some years in apple country — Massachusetts, Washington State, Michigan, Northern California and Up-State New York. Does the same climate so universally good for growing apples, create common characteristics among the people? I've experienced such a similarity between the cooking customs, temperament, attitudes and values of apple country people, whether on the east or west coast, whether in Canada or in the United States. Perhaps the link is not so much the climate as the rural ambience, plus an unconscious reaching-out and finding familiar traits and ways when far from home.

Part of the charm of the Cranberrie Cottage decade of my life is the setting. On the east side of the house is an old apple tree and along the boundary line behind the Baptist church are a dozen bright-blossomed sour-fruited wild apple trees, prickly blackberry brambles and asparagus gone wild. Down the road a bit, in Belle Isle, the records show that over two hundred years ago one Pierre Martin planted an orchard of apple trees he brought from Normandy. Behind the house, directly across the river, is Round Hill. In the mid 1900s there were over one hundred old trees there on a sixth generation farm. One, a Bishop Pippin, over two hundred years old, was ten feet in circumference and gave 33 barrels of apples a year. These and a multitude of things I learned during the Cranberrie Cottage years. Fate must have placed me in the midst of old *Acadie*, the cradle of apple culture in North America, as I could never have planned the richness of those years.

Over the centuries the apple has been much maligned as a controversial symbol of such things as seduction, sin, jealousy or discord. In some kitchens of the world the apple is highly prized as a gourmet delight while to others it is perceived as the fruit of the homely heartland of North America. It may well have been the "Forbidden Fruit" of the Garden of Eden although some Biblical scholars scorn the idea, suggesting rather the apricot or quince as the climate was not right for apple culture. If, indeed, the legendary fruit of the Tree of Knowledge was the apple, we know it has changed dramatically since then. In only one respect does the modern day apple resemble the symbol of Adam's downfall. It is irresistibly tempting.

The Apple Connection rests on that tempting, already proven quality of the apple. Whatever shape, colour or flavour and whatever form it takes in the kitchen, the apple continues to be irresistible. This is evidenced by the abundance of recipes that have survived through the years. No attempt is made to include all of the possible recipes; instead, I picked some of the tested best from all the provinces and states where the apple culture flourishes and some prized recipes from good cooks elsewhere. If there is an emphasis on some of my favourites — baked apples and apple pies — I make no apology.

The lack of traditional cookbook order is not by chance. The design, or lack of same, is a sort of outpouring of recipes, fact and folklore. My mother has an old scribbler with the same peculiar kind of order, and in it, either written, printed or pasted, are the recipes of her life. Her system introduced me to concoctions I would never have known had I relied only on an index or if, for example, all the pies and only pies were arranged together. I compromised, providing a table of contents that lists all recipes under various headings.

In all the **Connections** there are deliberate variations on old themes because some people find a recipe that works and never consider modifying it or trying something new. I didn't realize this approach to cooking was so common until after the cranberry book when women told me they had never and probably would never make anything but cranberry sauce and cranberry bread. Many of these same people now delight in being creative, not only with cranberries but with other foods, so I've included many suggestions in the apple book for minor recipe changes as well as new and more exotic ideas. Perhaps because this is the final book in the series, I've particularly enjoyed experimenting with apples, and hope that **The Apple Connection** will tempt others to be more inventive and versatile in the kitchen, with the fabled *pomme* — the ultimate temptation — the modern day ever adaptable, crunchy, juicy, sweet or tart, APPLE.

*   *   *

Another spring has come to the Annapolis Valley of Nova Scotia. The apple orchards are bedecked in deep pink buds about to bloom, and the early June air, though cool, is sweet with the bouquet of

xiv

spring. Once again the promise of plenty is renewed. Once again the connection with the Acadian past, and with the first apple blossoms in North America, is celebrated and honoured. And once again I have had the joy, the sweet and the bittersweet joy, of reliving some hitherto long forgotten happenings when I was a little girl, in a little village in Nova Scotia.

Cranberrie Cottage
June, 1985

About the author

During the first two decades of a distinguished academic career in the United States, Dr. Beatrice Ross Buszek was identified chiefly by her expanding reputation as a college professor and administrator. Her career might have progressed in professional and ivy-sheltered serenity into the 1980s but, in 1976, she bought a cottage on a riverfront property in the fertile Annapolis Valley of Nova Scotia, her native province.

On the property she discovered a cranberry bog and in the warm sunshine of early October as the cranberries ripened she gathered her first harvest. This led to the publication of **The Cranberry Connection**.

Dr. Buszek, whose unprofessorial name is Bebe, chose the mock thriller title as an acknowledgement of the success of other academics, notably English university dons, who have developed sideline careers writing mystery and adventure tales.

Bebe's latest book lures the reader to apple orchards and roadside stands. It is the most tempting adventure of all and marks the end of the **Connections** culinary series.

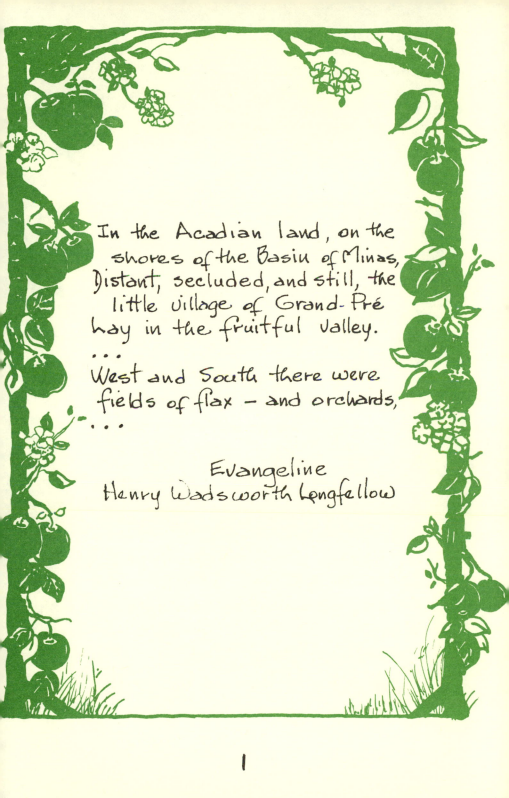

In the Acadian land, on the
    shores of the Basin of Minas,
Distant, secluded, and still, the
    little village of Grand-Pré
lay in the fruitful valley.
. . .
West and South there were
    fields of flax — and orchards,
. . .

            Evangeline
Henry Wadsworth Longfellow

All millionaires love
a baked apple
                Ronald Firbank

EXOTIC BAKED APPLES

Wash and core apples. Use
following ingredients to fill
apples, making as much as
needed for number of apples.

Filling:
Prepared mincemeat
mashed banana
dried chopped apricots
honey
4 T. light brown sugar
2 t. powdered mace
Juice of 1 small lemon

Prepare a deep buttered dish.
Stand apples. Fill, then put
a dab of butter on top of each
apple. Sprinkle lightly with
white sugar. Pour sherry over
apples, with enough in dish to
baste frequently. 350° - 1 hour

2

PORT ROYAL SOUP

2 cans consommé – 2 T. flour
2 tart, firm apples, cored, pared
1 heaping teaspoon curry powder
1 cup heavy cream
1 apple, sliced

Quarter the 2 apples and simmer in the consommé until tender. Strain and set aside. Combine the curry and flour with the cream and gently whisk. Season to taste. Add the puréed apple and combine with the consommé. Heat to boiling.

Serve in shallow bowls and garnish with thin slice of unpared apple, dusted lightly with curry.

Apple pie without cheese,
is like a hug, without
a squeeze.

3

The last week in September
has been celebrated in Ohio
since 1941 to honour the "voice
in the wilderness", Johnny Appleseed.

EARLY SETTLER PIE

Slice 6 medium apples and mix
with 3 Tablespoons molasses,
1/3 cup brown sugar, 1/4 teaspoon
each nutmeg and allspice and
1/8 teaspoon salt.
Heap apple mixture into a deep
greased baking dish and pour
about 1/2 cup hot water over
the top. Bake at 350° until
apples are tender. Remove and
top with biscuit dough and bake
until golden. Cool.
Serve warm or cold, with
heavy cream.

Now, also, thy breasts shall be
   as clusters of the vine
And the smell of thy nose like
   apples.   Song of Solomon
                         chap. 7, verse 8

4

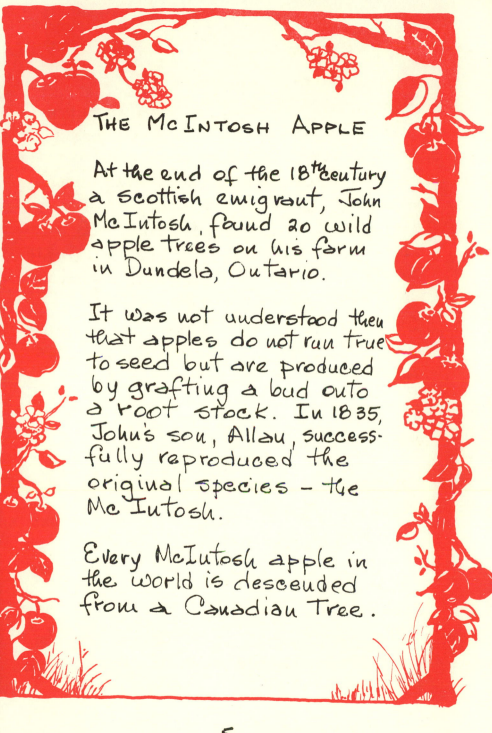

THE McINTOSH APPLE

At the end of the 18th century
a scottish emigrant, John
McIntosh, found 20 wild
apple trees on his farm
in Dundela, Ontario.

It was not understood then
that apples do not run true
to seed but are produced
by grafting a bud onto
a root stock. In 1835,
John's son, Allan, success-
fully reproduced the
original species – the
Mc Intosh.

Every McIntosh apple in
the world is descended
from a Canadian Tree.

NEIGHBORLY JAM

I usually make this jam several times in small amounts as I wait for two neighbors to call. One usually brings a bag of purple plums and the other an assortment of apples. My old tree provides some slightly bruised apples and the pear tree in the side yard, between the house and the church, drops lots of unsprayed, spotted, dwarfed pears. Use the following amounts as a guide but make-do, as I do, with what you have at the time.

1½ qts. pared, cored, chopped apples
1½ " halved, pitted purple plums
1 " pared, cored quartered pears

Wash fruit well before preparing as plum pits, apple and pear cores and skins are put aside, boiled gently

(continued

(continued)

about 15 minutes, then juice is
added to the fruit mixture.

Bring mixture to a boil. Simmer
until tender, then add about
3 pounds white sugar.
Stir well. Boil until thickened.
Ladle into sterilized jars.

KINNELON CHEESECAKE

Line a buttered pieplate with Graham Cracker crust.

Combine 1½ c. cran-apple sauce (or plain) with 2T. honey and 2T. brandy. Dissolve a ½ oz. pkg. plain gelatine (see pkg.). Mix into the apple sauce. Fold in 1 cup whipped cream.

Gently ladle into crust, saving some of graham crumb mixture to sprinkle over the top. Chill several hours before serving.

ANNAPOLIS VALLEY SLAW

Combine and blend:
  1/3 cup mayonnaise
  1 Tablespoon lemon juice
  1/2 teaspoon celery salt
  Dash white pepper

Make about 1/2 cup celery tops, sliced crosswise in thin shreds. Cut celery stalk in about 1½" pieces, slice lengthwise - 1/8" shreds (3 cups).

Put 1 large apple through a shredder and add 1/3 cup chopped walnuts.

Combine dressing, apple, celery and nuts and toss lightly. Chill.

Serve as a salad - especially good with baked chicken or roasted duckling.

I recollect,
        in early life
I loved the local
        doctor's wife.
I ate an apple
        ev'ry day
To keep the doctor
        far away.

MY FIRST LOVE

ANNAPOLIS VALLEY PUDDING

Butter a soufflé dish. Mix in it 1 c. brown sugar, ½ tsp. each nutmeg and cinnamon and 6 apples, sliced. Add ¼ c. water. Beat together ¼ c. melted butter, 2 egg whites and fold into ⅓ c. sifted flour and dash of salt. Spread over apple mixture. Cook at high heat for 10 mins. (450°), then 50 mins. at 350°. Watch that sides do not burn. Serve after slightly cooled, with a hot lemon sauce.

TAMPA TEMPTATION

1 c. corn oil   -   2 eggs
3 c. chopped, peeled apples
1 c. coconut   -   1 tsp. salt
2 c. sugar   -   1 tsp. soda
2 c. flour   - 3/4 c. broken nuts

Mix oil, eggs and sugar together.
Add dry ingredients and mix
well. Blend in apples, nuts
and coconut.
Bake 45 minutes at 350°
in buttered floured 13 x 9 pan.

Cool on rack, then frost.

Frosting:
1 - 8 oz pkg. cream cheese
1 stick margarine
2 Tablespoons vanilla
2 cups Confectioner's sugar

Mix well and spread over
the cake. Yummy!

12

APPLE - RHUBARB CRUNCH

1 cup cooked apples
2 cups cooked rhubarb
Juice and grated rind 1 small lemon
2 eggs — 1 T. corn starch
1/4 cup corn syrup
Scant 2 cups milk
1 tsp. vanilla extract
1/2 cup butter — 1 1/4 cups rolled oats
1 tsp. all-spice — 6 T. brown sugar

Combine apples, rhubarb and
lemon in a buttered shallow
baking dish. Make a custard
with the eggs, cornstarch,
syrup and milk. Remove from
heat, add flavouring and pour
custard over fruit mixture.
To the melted butter add rolled
oats, spice, sugar. Stir well.
Spoon over custard. Bake
at 325° for 20 minutes.
Serve warm or cold.

In 1937, the most popular jazz
dance was "the big apple."

14

APPLESAUCE CAKE

2 cups Apple sauce - 1 cup butter
2 cups brown sugar - 4 cups flour
2 teaspoons baking soda - 1 tsp. salt
1 teaspoon each cinnamon, nutmeg, cloves
1 cup each nuts, currants, raisins, figs,
                      dates or citron (4 c.)

Cream butter and sugar. Add
baking soda and apple sauce.
Stir into the mixture, the sifted
flour and spices. Fold in the
4 cups of nuts and fruits and
bake at 350° for 1½ hours.
Douse with sherry. Cover with
tight lid and store 2-3 months.
This cake can be used immediately and makes a lovely gift.

15

The story of the apple industry
is far richer than a mere recitation
of names, dates and places. It tells
of men and women who planted
and harvested, who dreamed
dreams and spun fragile hopes
for the future. The apple connection
was an integral part of the early
development of the New World.

DRIED APPLE STUFFING

1 cup dried apples — 1 onion
1 cup apple cider — salt, pepper
1 cup bread crumbs — mint leaves
1 Tablespoon bacon fat

Soak apples at least ten hours.
Sauté chopped onion in bacon
drippings, adding bread crumbs,
salt and pepper and Apples.

This stuffing is equally good
for poultry or pork. Baste
with cider, mixed with maple
syrup for an added gourmet
touch. Mint is optional.

During the 1960s, New York City was called "Fun City." After 1970 it was known as "the Big Apple"; ie, THE place!

TEMPTING RELISH

1 lb. apples, cored and chopped.
4 lbs. small green tomatoes, chopped.
1½ lbs. small to medium onions, "
Combine above with 1 cup of vinegar. Boil, then simmer about 30 minutes, gradually adding 8 chopped red chillies, 8 ozs. chopped dates and 1oz. dried ginger tied in a piece of cheese cloth. Cook another 30 minutes. Add 2 teaspoon salt, 1 pound sugar and 1 cup vinegar. Cook until thick. Remove ginger. Ladle into sterilized jars and seal. Do not use for two months.

"Apple" is the generic name for fruit.

APPLE CASSEROLE

This dish was served at a Bed and Breakfast in Santa Fe, New Mexico. It was so good that I asked for the recipe.

Combine according to the number to be served.
sliced peeled apples
chunks cooked ham
cooked rice

Cook in greased dish at 350° for about 40 mins. Top with butter dabs and blanched slivered almonds - return to hot oven for about 6-8 minutes. Serve!

HOLIDAY PARFAITS

Gently fold together cranberrie applesauce with whipped cream flavoured with nutmeg or almond. When stiff and well chilled, heap into parfait glasses.

See page 59 for Cranberrie Apple-sauce.

FRUIT WATER

"Fruit waters" were once served
to patients with fever as they
are "cooling, refreshing and mildly
stimulating" according to the
BOSTON COOKING SCHOOL COOKBOOK,
1896.
1 large tart apple, pared and cored.
1 T. sugar — 1 c. boiling water.
Fill apple with sugar and bake.
Mash. Pour boiling water over
mashed apple. Stand an hour.
Strain.

APPLE STUFFING

Chop 3 large stalks of celery including leaves. Add 2 large tart apples, quartered and cut in half and ¾ cup seedless raisins. Mix well. Amounts can vary according to size of bird. An Apple-celery combination is especially fine with roast duckling.

PICKLED APPLES

Combine:
½ c. cider vinegar, ½ c. water and ⅔ c. sugar. Tie in a bag, 1 T. pickling spices, and add to vinegar mixture. Slice 1 lemon, paper thin, add to above and bring to a boil. Simmer about 10 minutes. Add 1 can sliced apples, and ½ cup dried cranberries, blueberries or currants. Simmer a few minutes then set aside all night. In morning, bring again to a boil, simmer about 5 minutes. Remove spices. Ladle into prepared jars.

Bucks County Strudel

Sift together ½ c. flour and dash of salt. (Add another tablespoon of flour if needed).

Mix with 3 T. warm apple juice, 1 T. vegetable oil and 1 beaten egg. Knead on floured board (be stingy with flour) until smooth. Cover and stand aside.

Slice enough apples to fill a 9" crust. Crush ¼ cup slivered almonds. Mix together, then add ¼ cup dried blueberries or seedless raisins, 2 T. fine fresh bread crumbs and 1 T. light brown sugar.

In a large skillet, melt about 2 T. butter. Add to the apple mixture, gently turning over and over until heated through. Knead and roll out pastry. Place it on buttered baking sheet. Cover with apple mixture. Roll up and secure ends. Bake 30 mins. at 375°.

CALIFORNIA CHUTNEY

2 lbs. apples — 4 lbs. oranges
1 lb. onions — 1 lb. currants
2 tsp. ginger — 1 tsp. cayenne
3 pts. vinegar — 2 lbs. sugar

Chop onion and cook in small amount of water for 10 mins., then add chopped cored apples and cook another 15 mins. Peel orange, mince pulp and rind, keeping the juice. Combine onions, apples and oranges with currants, spices, half of vinegar and simmer 1 hour. Season to taste with salt,
Add sugar and remainder of vinegar. Cook until mixture thickens. Do not use for about 2 months and store in jars in cool place.

USE IDEA:
Use apple juice instead of water or stock in making split pea soup, chicken soup, or vegetable soup.

ROASTED APPLE PATTIES

2 large grated apples
1 can cooked spinach, 190g size.
2 eggs, beaten, salt, pepper to taste
1 pkg. cream cheese, 8oz, softened

Cook apples in the water from spinach.
When fruit is tender and water gone,
mix in the spinach, chopped fine.
Stir constantly. Add cheese, salt,
pepper and beaten eggs. When
well mixed, add about 1/2 cup
flour with 1/8 teaspoon finely diced
Rosemary.
Using deep skillet, with peanut oil,
add mixture 1 Tablespoon at a time.
Lightly brown each side and serve
hot around a pork roast.

23

APPLE KALAMAZOO

Cooking apples - sliced
¼ cup sugar - ¼ cup butter
Grated peel and juice of 1 orange
1 teaspoon Apple pie spice
8 slices white bread, remove crusts
½ cup butter - 1 Tablespoon sugar

Mix all except bread, butter and
1 Tablespoon sugar. Simmer until
Apples barely tender.
Break bread into bite size pieces
and sauté in ¼ cup butter. When
crisp, line bottom and sides of
greased casserole. Add the
apple mixture, dot with butter,
cover with bread bits, add
more butter and sprinkle with
sugar.
Bake about a half hour at
400°.

Serve with maple walnut
ice cream.

CORNELL SWEET POTATOES

3 large cooking Apples
6 medium sweet potatoes
2 Tablespoons butter - Salt
¾ cup Maple syrup

Preheat to 350°. Cook sweet
potatoes, covered, 20-30 minutes.
When potatoes are tender,
drain, peel and cut crosswise
slices at least ¼" thick.
Slice apples about ⅛" thick.

Place half of sweet potatoes
in a buttered casserole.
Add half the apples, half the
butter, syrup and salt. Repeat.

Cover and bake a half hour.
Remove cover and cook
another 12-15 minutes.

"Who so toucheth you, shal
  touche the aple of his owne eye"

25

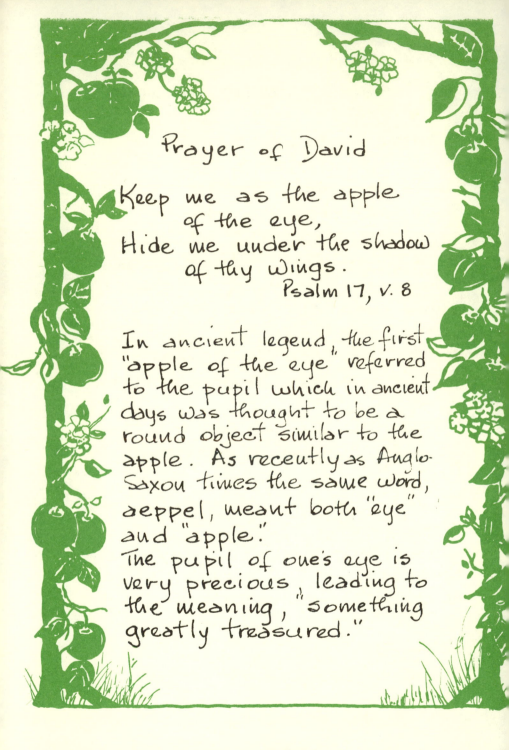

Prayer of David

Keep me as the apple
     of the eye,
Hide me under the shadow
     of thy wings.
                    Psalm 17, v. 8

In ancient legend, the first
"apple of the eye" referred
to the pupil which in ancient
days was thought to be a
round object similar to the
apple. As recently as Anglo-
Saxon times the same word,
aeppel, meant both "eye"
and "apple."
The pupil of one's eye is
very precious, leading to
the meaning, "something
greatly treasured."

26

The true fathers of the Nova Scotia apple industry were the post-Acadians, the New England Settlers, "the sons of Massachusetts, Rhode Island and Connecticut."

OKANAGAN SOUP

2 cups applesauce (sweeten to taste)
1 T. cornstarch
2½ cups apple juice
1 T. honey — 2 T. lemon juice
1 tsp. grated lemon rind
⅛ tsp. each nutmeg and cinnamon

Strain applesauce into saucepan. Dissolve cornstarch in apple juice and add to applesauce, along with remaining ingredients. Heat, stirring often, until clear and slightly thickened. Remove and chill. Serve cold with dollop of sour cream and fresh fruit — blueberries, strawberries or others. Serve as appetizer or dessert.

SOUR CREAM DRESSING

Combine in top of double-boiler,
2 tsp. each flour and sugar,
1 tsp. each dry mustard and salt,
and 1/4 tsp. cayenne. Beat 1 egg
yolk with 1/2 cup cider vinegar.
Cook about 12 minutes at low
heat. Add about 2 Tablespoons
melted butter. Cool.
Before using, fold into 1/2 cup
whipped sour cream.

In Ireland, the apple
tree is believed to
represent immortality.

CRUMBLE TOPPING
Crumble together:
1 cup lt. brown sugar — 1/2 cup butter
1 cup sifted flour — dash of salt

Use as topping for pies or
puddings.

"Her apple-blossom complexion."
Miss Mitford, 1824

28

QUICK APPLESAUCE SALAD

2 cups heavy apple sauce
1 cup cottage cheese
1 pkg. apricot (or lime) gelatin
3/4 cup boiling water

Combine applesauce and cheese.
Dissolve gelatin into the boiling
water (use boiling apple juice
if you have an opened can in
the 'frig.)
Fold two mixtures together.
Pour into a ring mold or a
square pan. Chill immediately.

Variation: Add 1 apple either
grated or chopped in fine pieces.

SOME SIMPLE SUGGESTIONS

ACORN APPLE ROUND

Arrange apple slices in spokelike fashion inside centre of acorn squash. Sprinkle with cinnamon and nutmeg. Bake.
Serve as side dish with pork and ham.

HOT CRANAPPLE RELISH

Mix cranberries, chopped apples and oranges, and walnuts together. Add spices and bake. Serve as side dish with ham or turkey

APPLES MEXICANA

Serve apple wedges with guacamole cheese spread as appetizer.

APPLE ARITHMETIC

1 pound apples	=	about 3 medium apples
about 5 pounds apples	=	4 quart basket
about 7 pounds apples	=	6 quart basket
45-48 pounds apples	=	1 bushel basket
1 medium apple	=	1 cup chopped apple
1 pound apples	=	3 cups diced apples
1 pound apples	=	1 1/2 cups applesauce
2 pounds apples	=	one 9-inch apple pie

ENGLISH DESSERT

Dip apple slices in lemon juice and sauté in butter on both sides. Sprinkle with sugar until apples are coated. Turn and sprinkle with nutmeg, turn and repeat. Remove apples carefully and arrange on a serving platter.

Add some apple juice to the pan, then heavy cream and a dab of butter. Heat slowly, then pour over apples. (Estimate amounts according to apples)

31

A REAL MAN'S QUICHE

Prepare -
About 1 cup chopped smoked ham
combined with 2 medium cored,
peeled and chopped apples and
12 ozs. Blue cheese. Heat in
top of double boiler. Add dash
salt and pepper and 1/4 cup milk,
when cheese mixture is
smooth.
Remove from heat and add
2 slightly beaten eggs.
Pour into unbaked shell
and bake about 55-60 mins.
at 350°.
Just before serving, grate
another small apple and mix
with finely chopped assorted
nutmeats, and sprinkle over
the top.

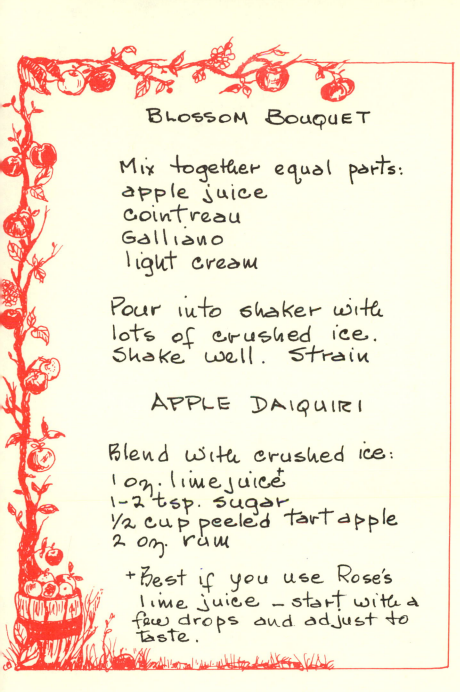

BLOSSOM BOUQUET

Mix together equal parts:
apple juice
Cointreau
Galliano
light cream

Pour into shaker with
lots of crushed ice.
Shake well. Strain

APPLE DAIQUIRI

Blend with crushed ice:
1 oz. lime juice⁺
1-2 tsp. sugar
½ cup peeled tart apple
2 oz. rum

⁺Best if you use Rose's
lime juice — start with a
few drops and adjust to
taste.

BURGUNDY APPLES

Select 4 firm apples with stalks. In deep saucepan, mix together 1 cup sugar with about ½ cup water. Bring to boil. Gently immerse the apples, cover and cook about 15 minutes. Add ¾ cup red Burgundy wine, uncover and gently cook another 15 minutes.

Remove apples, if tender, and cool them. Continue to boil syrup until thickened. Pour over the apples. Serve chilled. Vary recipe by adding pears.

34

PORT ROYAL FLAMBÉES

The apple seedlings brought to
Port Royal by the early explorers,
produced small sour apples
used to make cider. The fruit
in this recipe should be large,
firm and sweet.

Select apples with stems.
Carefully wash, then liberally
brush with lemon juice. Combine
   1 cup light brown sugar
   1 teaspoon cinnamon
   2 pints water
Boil until sugar is dissolved.
Add apples, cover, and
simmer until barely tender,
about 15 minutes. Drain.
Place on ovenproof platter.
Boil syrup until it is thickened.
Pour over the apples, then
top with ½-¾ cup rum.

Just before serving, ignite the
rum. Eat immediately.

Presidio Salad

2 cups grated apples, unpared
2 "   "   pears, unpared
1⅓ "   celery, sliced
2-3 T. drained horseradish
¼ cup sugar — ⅓ cup lemon juice
¾ cup sliced toasted almonds
dash of salt.
Combine and chill well.

Whip cream — about ¾ - 1 cup.
Just before serving, fold
fruit/horseradish mixture into
the whipped cream, using a
large serving bowl. Chill.

36

BAKED MACAROON APPLES

Mash some butter and light brown
sugar and stuff apples. Top
each apple with crushed
macaroons. Place in a buttered
baking dish (actually I usually
stuff apples after placing
them in buttered dish).
Serve when barely tender,
topping with whipped cream.
Bake at 350° for about an hour,
depending on size of apples.

"The apple grows so bright
and high, and ends its day
in apple pie."

"Année venteuse,
Année pommeuse."
     (lots of wind, lots
          of apples)

"they're apples in English,
apfels in German,
appils in Norwegian;
and eppels in Dutch -
and in any language,
they're delicious."

        Mme. Jehane Benoit

38

"so fruit that is shaken, or beat off a tree, With bruising in falling, soon faultie will be."
Thos. Tusser, 1573

THE CLASSIC NEW JERSEY STONE WALL PUNCH

1 qt. applejack — 1 qt. cider
1 qt. water
Combine and pour over ice-ring in punch bowl. Stir well. Garnish with thin slices of oranges and lemons, studded with cloves.
Makes about 30 servings.

One seedling raised about 1830 has resulted in thousands of Orange Pippin trees all over the world.

CALIFORNIA COLESLAW

3 large firm red apples, sliced
2 small fresh pineapple, diced
3 cups young cabbage, shredded
2 large carrots, grated

Prepare apples and brush with
2 Tablespoons lemon juice. Combine
next three ingredients, then add
apples, salt and pepper to
taste, 3/4 cup diced celery,
and about 10-12 finely sliced
green onions. Toss gently
while gradually adding sour
cream - just enough to coat.
Chill well and serve with
sour cream Dressing. (see page 28)

PER CAPITA CONSUMPTION IN U.S. (1980)

	Pounds
All apples (fresh and processed)	28.9
Fresh apples	16.7
Canned (including applesauce)	3.3
Juice	7.3
Frozen	0.6
Dried	1.0

MONTREAL SORBET

2 cups Cranberry Applesauce
Sugar to taste, about ½ cup
1 cup heavy cream
¾ cup port wine
½-¾ slivered toasted almonds

Combine and blend at medium speed. Fill container and place in freezer. Before mixture is frozen hard, remove, stir quickly and well, then replace in freezer.

41

DRIED APPLE RINGS

Wash, peel and core mature apples. Arrange slices in a single layer on baking sheet and dry in cool oven set at 'warm' or 120°, for 5-10 hours.

Turn once or twice. Slices should be dry on outside but moist inside.

Place dried apples in a loosely covered container for five days, tossing them at least once a day.

Store in cool, dry, dark place. Dried apples give "intense flavor to sweet and savory dishes, sautéed or not, in a little liquid."

Cidering gives a child instant gratification. Noel Perrin
Second Person Rural

42

CURRIED RICE
with APPLE

Cut apples into
chunks. Sauté in
3 Tablespoons butter
for 2 medium apples.
Add 1/4 teaspoon curry.
Gently mix together
and cook until tender

Fold into hot cooked
rice, seasoned to
taste.

APPLE PIE TIP
Before adding the
top crust, place a
few slices of process
sharp cheese on apples.

The Apple Pie Fair in Devon, England is held on Aug. 25th. Apple pies are sold and an Apple Pie Princess is crowned to honor the generosity of a 19th century farmer, George Hill.

(continued)

APPLES, ALMONDS and DATES

2 pounds Apples — 1 pound onions
1½ pounds stoned dates — 8oz. sugar
3 oz. chopped almonds
1 pint vinegar — 1 teaspoon each
   cayenne, salt, powdered ginger

Chop onions and bring to a boil. Add chopped apples and cook 15-20 minutes. Add all other ingredients except sugar and half of the vinegar. When mixture begins to thicken, add sugar and remainder of vinegar. Simmer until thick. Ladle into jars but set aside for at least a month before using.

44

Each year, Geo. Hill gave apple
windfalls from his orchards
to his workers and donated an
outsize Apple-pie, transported
on a donkey cart, to the village
fair. The ceremony is still
commemorated by villagers.

Reader's Digest, 1980

POMONA PIE

Prepare a baked flaky pastry crust.
Cool before adding apple filling.

Make a syrup of 1 cup light
brown sugar and 1 cup of water.
Add to this about 8 small
green apples, quartered. Cook
about 15-20 minutes or until
apples are tender but firm.

Remove apples with perforated
spoon and continue to boil
syrup until it is thick. When
cooled, pour syrup over the
apples that are now in cooled
pastry shell. Serve with whipped
cream, topped with grated lemon rind.

APPLE BLOSSOM SODA

Apple Juice, well chilled
Cranberry cocktail, chilled
Vanilla (or your favourite)
ice-cream

Into each chilled tall glass,
pour ¾ cup apple juice.
Gently add 1 large scoop of
ice cream. Top with cran-
berry cocktail* well chilled.

*Cranapple cocktail can be
substituted, or dry gingerale, with a couple maraschino
cherries.

46

APPLEBERRY RELISH

Combine 4 finely chopped apples with 1 cup finely chopped cranberries, 2 cups sugar and 2 Tablespoons candied ginger, diced very fine. Chill well before serving.

Mix applesauce, lemon juice and tomato sauce for a tangy barbeque sauce. Try it now!

NEW YORK STATE APPLES

GOOD SO MANY WAYS

THE APPLE OF THE
XIII OLYMPIC WINTER GAMES LAKE PLACID 1980

WINTER PIE

Make pastry for 2-crust pie. Combine 2 cups Applesauce with 1 cup each mincemeat and cranberry sauce. Dot with butter.

Line dish with pastry. Fill with apple mixture and top with lattice crust. Sprinkle with sugar. Bake about 50 mins. 350°

If the foliage is healthy, apples continue to grow in volume at a rate of about 2% per day until almost all apples drop or cool weather comes.

BAKED APPLES

Wash and core as many apples as you need. Pare about a ⅓ of the way down. Set in a shallow baking dish. Add about 1 Tablespoon sugar into each apple and top with a dab of butter. Pour some water to cover bottom of dish. Do not cover. Bake at 350° for 50-60 minutes - or until tender.

Use, as directed above, with the main dish. Vary with cinnamon sprinkled over top, or try some herbs, chopped fine. Mint leaves are an unexpected flavor, and lemon balm is also good.

The first apple plantings were brought to the U.S. from England in 1629.

48

CURRIED APPLE SOUP

2 large tart apples, chopped
1 large onion, minced
1/4 cup butter — 1 large banana, sliced
5 cups chicken stock
1/4 cup curry powder
Juice of 1/2 lemon — dash of salt
1/4 tsp. nutmeg
Optional: 2 T. Indian mango chutney

Saute apple and onion in butter
for 5 minutes. Add banana and
sauté slowly another 5 minutes.
Add curry powder, stir and cook
1 minute, then add stock, nutmeg,
lemon juice and chutney. Simmer
about 25 minutes. Salt to taste.
Chill well before serving.
Variation: Substitute dry white
wine for half the chicken stock.

Him by ~~fraud~~ I have seduc'd
from his creator ... with an
Apple.
                    Milton, 1667

49

West Virginia Apple sauce

Combine and chill 2 cups unsweetened apple sauce, 2 tbsp.
grated orange rind and 1 tablespoon
aromatic bitters.

Cider was often prescribed by
Physicians.

ORIENTAL APPLES

3 chopped apples
1 medium onion, sliced in rings
Butter
1 medium cabbage, shredded
½ cup each dark brown sugar
   and hot water
⅓ cup wine or cider vinegar

Sauté apples and onion in butter,
about 10 minutes. Add cabbage
and hot water. Cook about
25 minutes. Add vinegar and
sugar and serve hot.

Physicians regarded water as "cold,
slow and slack of digestion".

The Gravenstein was the most
famous apple of the 20th century.
Originally from Germany, it came
to the New World from England.

APPLE PANCAKE GÂTEAU

Make your favourite pancake batter.

Peel and core 1½ lbs. apple. Cut
into thick slices. Grate rind
of ½ a lemon and add along with
the lemon juice. Soften in
saucepan over low heat. When
soft, beat gently with wooden
spoon, add dash of cinnamon
and sweeten to taste.
Cook pancakes.
Make alternate layers of
pancakes and filling, ending
with an uncovered pancake.
Sprinkle mixture of sugar and
cinnamon over top.
Serve with a bowl of
whipped cream.

"A goodly apple rotten at the heart"
          Merchant of V. I, iii, 102   1596

51

SWEET - SOUR MEATBALLS
(with apples and red cabbage)

Use a Dutch oven or large saucepan.
Mince 1 medium onion and sauté
in about 1 Tablespoon butter. Add
    ½ cup vinegar
    3 cloves - 1 bay leaf
    1 teaspoon caraway seed
Cover and simmer about 5 minutes.

Mix together
    1 pound lean ground beef
    1 beaten egg - ¼ tsp. nutmeg
    ¼ c. fine dry bread crumbs
    ¼ c. chopped raisins
    Grated rind of ½ lemon
    1 tsp. salt - ¼ tsp. pepper
Shape into small balls.
Add to first mixture. Cook,
stirring gently, about 10 minutes.

(Some people prefer to tie the
spices in a bag, but I prefer
to mix them into the mixture and
then remove cloves and bay leaf)

(Continued)

SWEET-SOUR MEATBALLS
(cont'd)

Combine
  4 c. chopped red cabbage
  2 T. light brown sugar
  2 tart apples, peeled + diced
  Salt and pepper

Put apple mixture in bottom
of large saucepan. Add meat
balls and the sauce. Cover
and simmer about 45 minutes

Serve meat balls on platter
and surround with apple/
cabbage mixture.

FRENCH ACADIAN SOUP

2 tart apples, pared, cored and
                          chopped.
2 medium onions, chopped.
Sauté onions in 2 T. butter.
When onion is tender, add apples
and sauté about 1 minute.

Cut up 2 haddock fillets (1-1½lbs)
into bite-size pieces, adding
½ pint stock, salt and pepper to
taste, 1½ cups cider and fresh
Rosemary. Simmer gently a half
hour. Just before serving,
remove the Rosemary.

This soup is a favourite in
Louisiana among the French
Acadian descendants from
Nova Scotia (Acadia in 1755)

The original plantings of apple
trees in Nova Scotia was in
Port Royal in 1606, according to the
writings of Lescarbot, one of the
earliest explorers.

54

APPLE-PORK PIE

Mix together 3 grated apples and about 1 pound finely minced fresh pork, salt and pepper, and your favourite herb — thyme is good and Rosemary is always good with pork — parsley can be added.

Roll out pastry for 2 crusts. Fill with above mixture and spread evenly. Beat 1 egg yolk and brush the rim of the pastry so top and bottom will stay together. Top with crust and brush with remainder of the egg yolk.

Bake at 400° for 20 minutes, then at 375° for 30 minutes. Serve hot.
(A flaky pastry is best)

"He who flatters the cook never goes hungry."
Proverb

55

Apples - one of the most widely distributed of tree fruits. Cultivation seems to correspond with the Teutonic and Anglo-Saxon races.

APPLE BRAN SALAD

2 c. cubed unpared red apples
½ c. lemon lowfat yogurt
½ c. thinly sliced celery
½ c. red grapes, halved and seeded
Fresh snipped parsley - about 2 T.

Gently stir together. Cover and chill well. Just before serving time, fold in ½ cup All-Bran or Bran Buds cereal. Serve on crisp lettuce leaves.
(per serving - 70 calories)

The Norsemen believed the apple to be the rejuvenating food of their gods. The goddess, Iduna, was said to keep a box of apples from which the gods, when they felt old age approaching, had only to taste to become young again.

VARIATION ON A GAZPACHO

Peel, core and slice about 5-6 cooking apples.
Combine apples with juice and rind of 1 orange, 1 large can tomatoes, 2 cups stock, 1 T. sugar, 1/4 t. sweet basil, dash of salt and pepper.

At boiling point, immediately turn to lowest heat and simmer gently about 1 hour. Stir well. Serve in soup mugs.

Carbonized specimens of apples were found in the tombs of the Pharaohs.

57

"Apple Water, otherwise called Sider." 1606
Cider came from Normandy after the conquest. It was the staple drink of the poor whose only alternative was water.

TIPSY TORTE

Make plain pastry, substituting 1 Tablespoon brandy for 1 of water. Cook and cool.

4 Tart apples, sliced
½ cup sugar - 1 cup water
½ cup apricot jam -
2 Tablespoons lemon juice
2 Tablespoons brandy

Combine sugar, jam, water and juice. Heat to a boil, then strain through a sieve. Return mixture to the pan, add sliced apples. Gently simmer about 10 minutes but do not cover. Turn once with wooden spoon. Cool. Gently stir in brandy. Heap into cooked, cooled shell.

BELLE ISLE SOUP

2 sweet apples, pared, cored
and sliced
1 potato and 2 small onions,
pared and chopped and sauteed
in 1 T. butter until barely tender.
Add 2 cups vegetable water,
dash salt and pepper. Cover
and simmer about 15 minutes.
Add apples and cook until
all are tender. Stir often.
Serve hot or cold, topped
with a dollop of cream and
chives.

CRANBERRIE APPLESAUCE

Cook pared chopped apples, about
6, until barely tender. Add 1cup
cranberries. Cook until they
burst. Add ¾ cup sugar - to
taste, and 1 Table spoon lemon
juice and sprinkle with nutmeg.
Chill before serving.

TURKEY TEMPTER

Toss turkey cubes, yogurt, chopped unpared apples, and broken nutmeats together in a bowl. Serve in pita bread.

Garnish with additional apples, sliced and sprinkled with cinnamon.

APPLE-IZED TEA

Combine apple juice and instant tea; add cinnamon stick — guaranteed to warm you for winter snow-in days.

An apple is gold in the morning, silver at noon and lead at night.

(Editor's contribution)

60

ANNAPOLIS VALLEY ICE CREAM

Core and slice 6 red apples and
smooth 1 cup gooseberries. Add
1 cup sugar and ½ cup water
and cook until tender. Puree. Cool.

Beat ½ pint fresh coffee cream
until stiff. Gently fold it into the
fruit mixture. When nearly
frozen, beat again and repeat
several times. Ladle into
freezing tray.

NORTHFIELD PIE

Combine, bring to a boil and simmer about 5 minutes, covered:

1½ cups raisins
1½ cups shredded carrots
1 cup water (or apple juice)

Mix together and add to boiling mixture:

¾ cup sugar
1 Tablespoon cornstarch
1 teaspoon cinnamon
¼ teaspoon ground cloves

Cook, stirring gently, 5 minutes.

Remove from heat and stir in 2 Tablespoons butter until melted. Now add:

2 apples, peeled, cored and chopped
1 navel orange, finely chopped

Stir well, then cool.

Bake in 2-crust pie, about 45 minutes at 400°. Crust should be golden. Cool on pie rack.

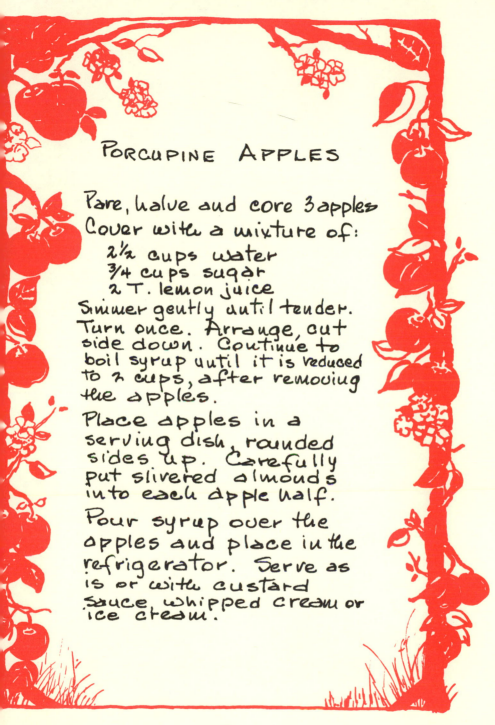

PORCUPINE APPLES

Pare, halve and core 3 apples
Cover with a mixture of:
  2½ cups water
  ¾ cups sugar
  2 T. lemon juice
Simmer gently until tender.
Turn once. Arrange, cut
side down. Continue to
boil syrup until it is reduced
to 2 cups, after removing
the apples.

Place apples in a
serving dish, rounded
sides up. Carefully
put slivered almonds
into each apple half.

Pour syrup over the
apples and place in the
refrigerator. Serve as
is or with custard
sauce, whipped cream or
ice cream.

SQUASHED APPLES

Wash and core 6 large tart firm baking apples. Scoop out a large cavity with the core.

Place apples in a buttered baking pan and into each cavity put a dab of butter, lemon rind and sugar.

Pour enough water with 2 T. cooking sherry to make ½" of liquid.

Squash can be cooked, from garden, but I use frozen squash in this recipe.
(Add sausage for light supper)
Mix squash with ¼ tsp. each nutmeg and pepper and salt to taste. Stir in 2-3 T. of sherry, ½ cup heavy cream and 4 T. butter. Blend in mixer.
Remove liquid from apple pan. Fill each one with squash, dot with butter and nutmeg and return to hot oven about 10 mins.

64

APPLE GINGER

Pare, core and chop enough apples
to weigh 2½ pounds, put in large
kettle and add:

   1½ lbs. brown sugar
   1½ lemons, juice and rind
   ½ ounce ginger root
   ½ teaspoon salt

Add enough water to keep apples
from burning. Cover and cook
slowly about 4 hours, stirring
frequently, adding water when
needed. Store in sterilized
glasses. Apple Ginger will keep
for several weeks.

SAVANNAH SALAD
A Tropical jellied Apple salad

1 pkg. lemon-flavour gelatin
1 cup each hot and cold apple juice.
1 T. lemon juice + grated rind
     of 1 lemon (or orange)
1 diced, unpeeled red apple
½ cup each chopped celery,
    broken walnuts, sliced dates

Dissolve gelatin in hot water, add cold water and juice. Chill until thickened then fold in remaining ingredients. Turn into 5-cup oiled mold. Chill until firm. Unmold and garnish with greens. Serve with sour cream dressing. (combine equal amounts dairy sour cream and mayonnaise. Sprinkle with grated citrus peel)

66

GRANDMA'S COOKIES

4 cups flour
2 tsp. baking soda
1 cup margarine
2-2/3 cups lt. brown sugar
2 eggs
2 cups chopped unpared apples
1/2 cup milk
1/2 tsp. salt
1 tsp. each cloves and nutmeg
2 tsp. cinnamon
1 cup chopped walnuts
1 cup raisins

Cream shortening, sugar, spices
and eggs. Blend thoroughly.
Combine flour, salt and soda.
Stir in 1/2 flour mixture, adding
apples, walnuts and raisins.
Add milk and remainder of flour
mixture. Drop on cookie sheet,
using tablespoon.
Bake at 375° for 10 minutes.
Glaze while hot.
(See page 131 for Glaze recipe)

VALENTINE PIE

6 sour sliced apples
2 Tablespoons red cinnamon hearts
¾ cup sugar — 3 Tablespoon flour
¼ tsp. salt — ¼ c. water - 3 T. butter

Prepare unbaked bottom crust.
Fill with sliced apples. Heat the
water, add cinnamon hearts and
stir until dissolved. Mix together
the sugar, salt and flour, add
to cinnamon water and cook
until thickened. Pour over the
apples, dot with butter.
Crumble dough over the top
and bake 10 minutes at 450°, then
about 40 minutes at 350°

68

APPLE CUSTARD PIE

5 to 6 Apples (Jonathans, Romes, Golden Delicious, Winesaps)
1 c. Sugar - 2 T. flour - ½ tsp. salt
½ tsp. Cinnamon - 2 Eggs
Mix dry ingredients. Beat eggs in cup and fill with cream or milk. (use whole milk). Arrange apples in quarters to form a circle in pastry. fill pie plate. Cover with sugar mixture, then pour in the milk and egg mixture.

Set oven at 450° but begin to bake at 350° until apples and custard are done. (Best not to use fast cooking apples).

"The cold was so intense that the Cider was divided by an axe and measured out by the pound."

Reference to early days at Port Royal, N.S.
            Samuel de Champlain, 1605
                        Diary

69

New York State Apple regions

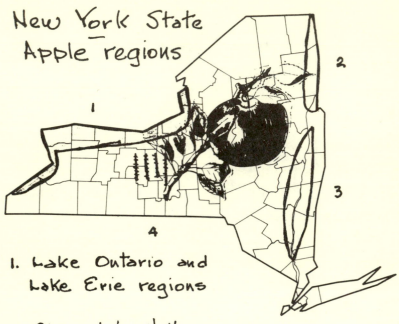

1. Lake Ontario and Lake Erie regions

2. Champlain Valley region

3. Hudson Valley region

4. Finger Lakes region

Large forests of wild apples in the Northeastern Himalaya Mountains suggest apples may have originated there. However, crab apples are native to North America and elsewhere, making origin of apples obscure.

APPLE BERRY CAKE

Preheat oven 300°
½ cup Apple sauce
¼ cup light brown sugar
¼ cup butter
¾ cup flour
1 teaspoon bicarbonate soda
¼ teaspoon nutmeg
¼ teaspoon cinnamon
⅓ cup dried blueberries

Cream butter and sugar, then
add the soda, applesauce
and flour, sifted with spices.
Gently stir in dried blueberries.

Spoon into a greased cake
pan and bake about 1 hour.

"The apple had done little for me, if
Eve had not done the rest."
ALL FOR LOVE, 1829

OUT OF THE CLOSET

Take pippins and pare and cut off
the tops of them pretty deep.
Then take out as much of your
apple as you can take without
breaking your apple, then fill your
apple with pudding-stuff, made
with cream, a little sack, marrow
(from bone), grated bread, eggs,
sugar, spice and salt. Make
it pretty stiff. Put it into the
pippins, lay the tops of the
pippins upon the pippins again,
stick it through with a stick
of cinnamon. Set as many upright in your dish as you can,
and so fill it up with cream,
and sweeten it with sugar and
mace, and stew them.

15th century recipe.

In early days Apple seeds were
called "pips".

72

"There's cold chicken inside it,"
replied the Rat briefly...
"Ou, stop, stop," cried the Mole in
ecstasies: "This is too much!"
                    Kenneth Grahame

CHICKEN-STUFFED APPLES

6 firm baking apples, peeled about
    ¼ down. Remove cores.
Place in baking dish, cover and bake
about 30 minutes at 350°. Add a
scant amount, in bottom of baking
dish.   of water
Remove from oven and gently
stuff with a mixture of:
1 cup cooked diced chicken
1 tsp. salt, dash of pepper, ⅛ tsp. cloves
⅓ cup fine bread crumbs. Top
with 2 T. melted butter, 1 tsp. sugar.
Bake another 20 minutes or
until apples are fork tender,
and retain their shape. Adjust
heat so apples will not mush.
Serve hot or cold. I like
this recipe served cold with
greens.

73

Who is the "black sheep" of the
apple family?
"His name is "hard cider" - without
a vestige of social standing, cast-
ing a blot upon the escutcheon
of the noble apple family." Hard
cider was, at various times,
attacked by pulpit and press and
"well deserved such treatment."

SPICED CRAB APPLES

Select firm crab apples with
stems. Insert 2 or 3 whole cloves
in each apple. Make a syrup of:
   3 pounds sugar —
   2 cups cider vinegar —
   2 ounce stick cinnamon —

Boil until quite thick. Place a few
apples in the syrup, turn and
cook until tender. Remove and
place in sterelized jrs.
Continue as above until all apples
are used. Boil syrup down,
pour over apples and seal.

"He is but a withered little
    Apple-John." Wash. Irving, 1882

74

APPLE JELLY

Slice apples into quarters but do not peel or core. Barely cover with water - about 2 cups water to 4 cups fruit. Boil until soft. Pour into jelly bag and drip overnight. Do not squeeze.

To 2 cups juice add 2 cups sugar and juice of a small lemon. Boil until syrup jells, skimming often. Ladle into jars and top with parafin.

Variation: Make mint jelly, letting sprigs of fresh mint soak in liquid while it nears boiling point. Let tiny pieces of mint leaves remain in the jelly but remove larger sprigs.

Liberty Hyde Bailey, famous horticulturist from Cornell University in Ithaca, N.Y., gave a talk in 1902 describing the dwarf apple trees in France.

20 carloads of the old Acadian apple trees were shipped to Philadelphia, Pa. to make tool handles, in 1919.

STUFFED CHICKEN BREASTS

Prepare as many boned chicken breasts as you will need. Make an "incision" 3/4 of way through each one. Beat each breast between waxed paper using a potato masher. Sprinkle with salt, pepper and minced sage. (or sweet basil)

Chop apples and celery and grate some cheddar cheese. Mix well. Stuff each boned breast and then secure with toothpicks. Dip chicken into a mixture of beaten eggs and bread crumbs and minced herbs. Fry in hot oil for about 8 to 10 minutes on each side.

APPLE BROTH

Combine apple juice, chicken broth and lemon juice. Serve with crackers as luncheon appetizer.

CHICKEN NORMANDY

Poach boned chicken breasts in apple juice; stir in cream and seasoning when chicken is cooked. Serve with fresh apple wedges.

JOSÉ APPLE SEED

Combine equal parts Tequila and apple juice. Pour into ice-filled glass and add slice of lime.

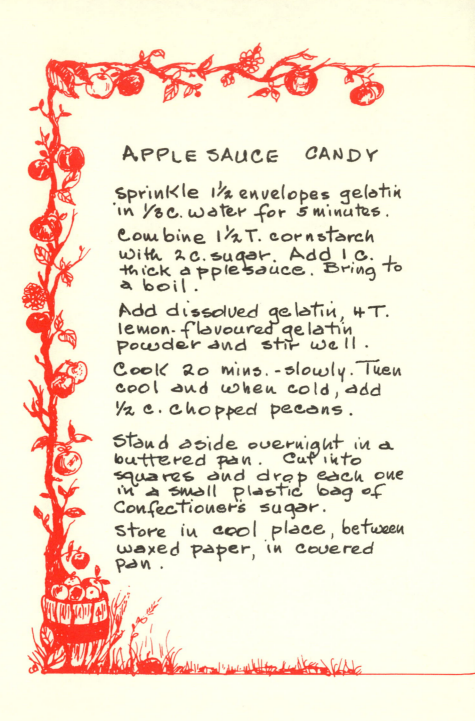

APPLE SAUCE CANDY

Sprinkle 1½ envelopes gelatin in ⅓ c. water for 5 minutes.

Combine 1½ T. cornstarch with 2 c. sugar. Add 1 c. thick apple sauce. Bring to a boil.

Add dissolved gelatin, 4 T. lemon-flavoured gelatin powder and stir well.

Cook 20 mins. - slowly. Then cool and when cold, add ½ c. chopped pecans.

Stand aside overnight in a buttered pan. Cut into squares and drop each one in a small plastic bag of Confectioner's sugar.

Store in cool place, between waxed paper, in covered pan.

ANN ARBOR APPLE SLAW

Combine and blend well:
½ cup mayonnaise
⅓ cup orange juice
2 Tablespoons sugar
Dash salt and pepper
½ cup wine or herb vinegar

Shred 2 tart apples. Select a
small red cabbage and use half
of it. Remove core and shred,
Now slice the rest of the
cabbage crosswise in shreds.
Mince about ⅓ cup green pepper
and chop ½ cup cranberries.
Combine all ingredients with the
dressing. Toss lightly and
chill. Serve with cold suppers.

The first Apple Blossom Festival in Nova Scotia, in 1933, was created to "internationally publicize the beauties of the orchards of Nova Scotia in bloom and to invite their fellow citizens throughout Canada as well as friends and neighbors from the U.S., to view this annual miracle."

APPLE SHERBET

Peel and core 5 apples and puree in a blender. This should make about 2 3/4 cups. Combine with 1 cup maple syrup (or simple syrup), 1/4 teaspoon nutmeg, and 1/3 cup Calvados. Freeze, but before it is too firm, fold in 1/2 cup finely chopped apple.

"La bonne table contribue puissament au bien-être."

80

SCOTTISH SQUARES

Line a buttered cake pan with a
mixture of:
  1/3 cup oatmeal, 1/3 cup flour,
  1 1/2 oz. light brown sugar and
  3/4 cup melted butter.
Top this with:
  2 apples, cored and sliced,
  3 T. honey, 1 T. butter and
  2 T. melted apple jelly.

Bake at 350° for 30 minutes.
Reduce to 325° and cook
another 15-20 minutes. Cut
when cool.

"Poor Richard was to me as an eldest son, the apple of my eye."
Scott, 1816

DETROIT APPLE GLAZE —

1 cup Apple juice
2 T. butter — 2 T. Vinegar
½ cup dark corn syrup
1 tsp. grated orange rind
2 Tablespoons orange juice
½ teaspoon ground ginger
4 Apples - pared and sliced

WITH SPARE RIBS

Cook spareribs about 1 hour at 450°. Drain.

Arrange layers of ribs, sliced apples and mixture of all other Glaze ingredients. Cover. Bake another hour at 350°, then remove cover. Bake longer until well browned. You may wish to baste with corn syrup.

82

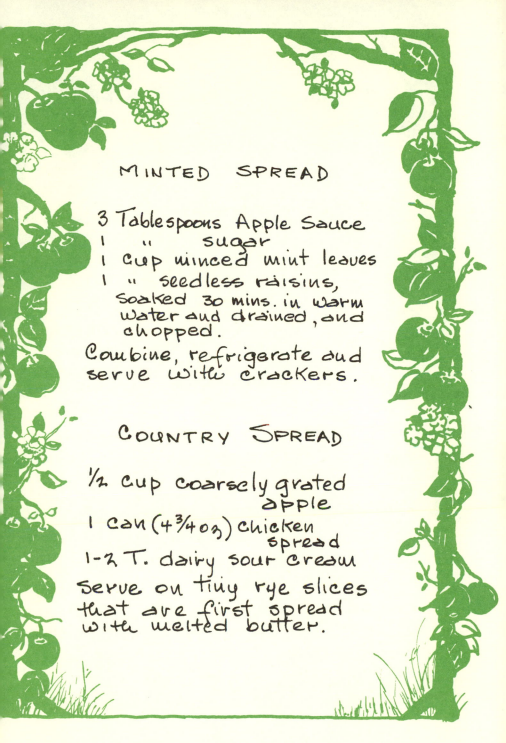

MINTED SPREAD

3 Tablespoons Apple Sauce
1   "   sugar
1 cup minced mint leaves
1 " seedless raisins,
   Soaked 30 mins. in warm
   water and drained, and
   chopped.
Combine, refrigerate and
serve with crackers.

COUNTRY SPREAD

½ cup coarsely grated
                apple
1 can (4¾ oz) chicken
                spread
1-2 T. dairy sour cream
Serve on tiny rye slices
that are first spread
with melted butter.

83

MICHIGAN APPLE DUMPLINGS

①
4 cups sifted flour
2 cups sour cream
1 teaspoon soda
Pinch of salt

<u>OR</u>

②
4 cups sifted flour
Butter, size of an egg
Pinch of salt
2 level tsp. baking powder
Milk to make stiff batter

Fill dumplings with:
8 apples, sugar, cinnamon, butter

Peel and halve apples, remove cores,
fill with sugar, sprinkle with spice
and dot with butter. Put halves
together. Mix and roll out dough
on floured board. Cut squares
and wrap one around each
apple. Seal edges with milk and
a pinch. Drop into boiling water,
cover tightly, serve in 15 minutes,
with heavy cream.

McIntosh Treats

2 large firm apples
1 tube buttermilk biscuits
⅓ cup melted butter (or margarine)
½ cup sugar — 1 tsp. cinnamon
¾ cup water.

Peel apples and cut them into
ten wedges. Dip into cinnamon-
sugar mixture. Roll each biscuit
thin, then carefully roll it around
apple wedge.
Grease a 9x13 pan. Brush the
melted butter over the top.
Sprinkle with remaining sugar-
cinnamon mixture.
Add water into baking pan.
Bake about 25 minutes at 425°.

The CORTLAND is a large apple
with firm, crisp white flesh that
stays white when cut. Parentage:
'Ben Davis' x 'McIntosh'.
Originated in New York State.

LUNENBURG SALAD

2 large apples, diced small.
Small fresh cabbage, sliced thin.
Toss lightly with about ¼ cup
basil vinegar (or cider), 1 T.
French mustard, 2-4 T. peanut
oil, salt and pepper.
Serve with sprigs of fresh
basil, if in season.

According to the Bible, the
Apple was the first fruit in
the world. If this is so, it
was not the cultivated apple
of today.

The apple is the "most important of the pome fruits." The fruit of the genus Pyrus is known to the botanist as a pome. Sometimes the apple is grouped into the genus Malus. They are related but will not inter-hybridize.

APPLE and QUINCE MARMALADE

Wash quince and remove blossom end. Cut in small pieces, barely cover with water and cook until tender. Rub through a sieve. Cook an equal amount of apples in the same way. Combine pulp, measure for measure. Add sugar, allowing two-thirds as much sugar as pulp. Cook slowly until thick and clear, about 25 to 30 minutes. Ladle into sterilized jars and seal.

In 1937, the Annapolis Valley Apple Blossom Festival Queen attended the annual Shenandoah Valley (Va) Festival - another sweet connection.

QUICK APPLE CAKE

Mix together ¾ cup peanut oil and
2 cups white sugar. (You can use
other oils, corn, etc.)
Add 2 beaten eggs.
Sift together 2 cups flour, 1 tsp.
salt and 1 tsp. soda.
Blend in the oil and sugar mixture.
Stir well. Fold in ¾ cup broken nuts.
Add 3 cups chopped, peeled apples.
Bake in buttered dish for 1 hour
at 350°.

GLAZE:
1 cup Confectioner's Sugar
1 Tablespoon butter — 1 Tablespoon milk
1 Tablespoon corn syrup

'The BIG APPLE' was a term originally used by U.S. Jazz players
in 1930s to mean any large city,
this planet or any large place,
especially up North.

Orig. Handbook of Harlem Jive
Dan Burley, 1944

APPLE-WALNUT SYRUP

2 c. apples sliced and peeled
¼ c. chopped walnuts - 3 T. butter
½ tsp. cinnamon - 1 c. Karo syrup

Melt butter, add nuts briefly.
Remove nuts and add remaining
ingredients. Cover and simmer
10 mins. Remove lid, simmer 3 more
mins. Remove from heat, add nuts.
Serve on ice cream, waffles,
custard, pancakes- you name it!

89

ROSE GERANIUM APPLES

(Core apples carefully)
Peel the top third of 6 CORTLAND apples. In a large skillet add the apple peelings, 1 cup sugar, 1 cup rose geranium flavoured apple juice and 1 cup water. Boil about 12-15 minutes, then cool slightly.
Place apples upright and in centre of each, place 1 or 2 rose geranium leaves lightly buttered. Cover with the cooked syrup, basting or turning frequently. Cook in medium oven until apples are barely tender and hold their shape.

(Add about 6 rose geranium leaves to 1 quart apple juice (or cider) and set aside, tightly covered, for 3-4 weeks.)

With apples, as with all agricultural products, Marketing is the name of the game.

90

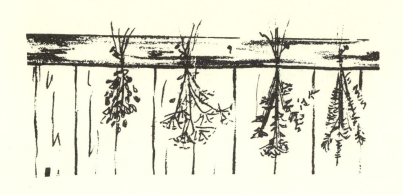

OLD FASHIONED DRIED APPLES

Pare, quarter, core and slice apples. Spread outside in the sun on a clean cloth. Cover with cheesecloth.
At sunset, bring inside and repeat for about a week until apples are leathery and brown. Place in brown paper bags and hang in dry attic. Be sure the paper bags are well tied.

"A plump, rosy-cheeked ... apple-faced young woman."
                    Dickens, 1848

91

APPLESAUCE TEMPTATION

Topping:
2 cups apple sauce
1 tsp. cinnamon - dash nutmeg
1/4 cup lt. brown sugar
1 tsp. lemon juice - 2 T. brandy

6 slices pound cake
Whipped cream

Combine topping ingredients.
Cut pound cake in 1/2-inch
slices. Toast golden brown
on each side. Ladle applesauce mixture on each
toasted slice. Garnish with
whipped cream.

The Romans were said to preserve whole apples in jars of honey. The elite served apples as dessert.

STUFFING for POULTRY or PORK

3 large apples, diced
1/2 cup celery, chopped
1/4 pound butter - 2 T. sugar
3/4 cup apple juice - salt
2 T. Summer savory
1/2 cup cranberries, chopped
6 slices cracked wheat bread
     (toasted and cubed)

Melt butter. Combine sugar, a dash of salt, apples, celery and savory. Simmer in the butter about 5 minutes. Toss lightly with bread cubes, adding just enough apple juice to make mixture moist. Add cranberries. (Cranberries add a twangy touch but can be omitted). Double recipe for a 10-12 pound bird or roast.

BRANDIED PRESERVE

Barely cover with water and simmer until tender, about 2 quarts sliced apples. Cool slightly and mash.
Combine 1½ lbs. sugar with juice and grated rind of two lemons. Boil until thickened. Add ¼ cup brandy. Fold in the mashed apples. Ladle into prepared jars.

What was the Sodom or Dead Sea Apple?
It was said to grow near Sodom (Josephus) and was fair in appearance but turned to smoke and ashes when plucked.

GARDEN CHUTNEY

3½ lbs. Apples - 3½ lbs. pears
2 lbs. green tomatoes - 2 lbs. onions
1 lb. small zucchini - salt
8 ozs. seedless raisins
8 ozs. brown sugar
1½ pints vinegar - 2oz. pickling spice
(tied in cotton bag)

Combine all except sugar and
salt, using half of vinegar. Boil,
then simmer until tender. Add
sugar, salt and remainder of
vinegar. Cook until thick, then
remove spice bag.

Note: Apples, pears, tomatoes, zucchini
and onions should be finely
chopped.

APPLE PIE ORDER

This is a corruption of the French phrase nappe plié meaning "folded linen." It refers to dinner napkins so it is quite natural that it found its way to the kitchen.

The phrase is now commonplace yet there is controversy as to its origin. One story comes out of early New England where a colonial housewife always baked seven pies for the week ahead. When the pies were baked and cooled she arranged them in order on the pantry shelf. First was Monday's pie, and so on. She was precise, determined they would be in apple-pie order.

(continued...)

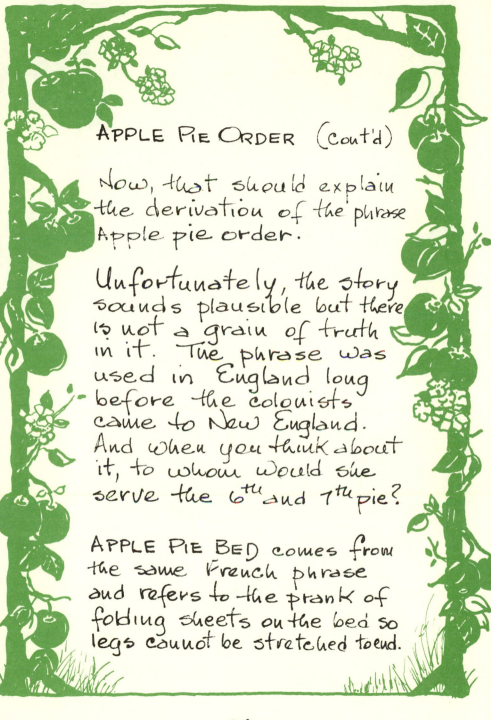

APPLE PIE ORDER (Cont'd)

Now, that should explain the derivation of the phrase Apple pie order.

Unfortunately, the story sounds plausible but there is not a grain of truth in it. The phrase was used in England long before the colonists came to New England. And when you think about it, to whom would she serve the 6th and 7th pie?

APPLE PIE BED comes from the same French phrase and refers to the prank of folding sheets on the bed so legs cannot be stretched to end.

ANOTHER OLD RECIPE

① Combine dried apples, figs, blueberries and pears with raisins and your favourite spices. Pound well in a mortar and color with saffron.
Mix with pastry and bake well.

② Peel, core and slice apples. Put in pan, dot with butter, light brown sugar and sweet white wine. Simmer until tender, with lid on. Remove from heat and cool. Slice some mild cheese and put apple mixture between 2 slices of cheese.. Flavour with sugar and cinnamon.

Apple-John or John-Apple (ripens on St. John's day in Brittain and Holland). Said to keep 2 years and to be in perfection when shrivelled and withered.

The golden apple, inscribed "for the fairest," was fabled to have been thrown by the God of Discord into the assembly of the Gods.

Apple of Discord

EXOTIC APPLE RELISH

½ cup unsweetened apple sauce
2 Tablespoons each:
tiny capers, stuffed olives,
pitted black olives - finely chopped
Combine with ½ cup mayonnaise
and 2 Tablespoons fresh minced
parsley.

By the end of the 30's, the
number of apple trees had
lessened by half a million,
in Nova Scotia.

99

APPLE BERRY MUFFINS

1¾ c. all-purpose flour - ½ tsp. salt
¼ c. lt. brown sugar - ½ tsp. baking soda
1½ tsp. baking powder - ¼ c. butter
1 egg - ¾ c. sweetened apple sauce
¾ c. milk - ¼ tsp. cinnamon
1 c. fresh blueberries or cranberries
2 T. flour - Cinnamon Sugar

Sift together first five ingredients.
Combine beaten egg, melted butter,
milk, applesauce and spice. Mix
two mixtures together.

Toss berries (fresh or frozen)
with small amount of flour; fold
into the batter. Spoon into the
greased muffin tins. Sprinkle
with a mixture of ¼ cup sugar
and ½ teaspoon cinnamon.

Makes about 12 muffins.

An Apple Polisher: one who curries
favour by flattery.

ADAM'S APPLE

Combine and stir over glass
of crushed ice :
1½ oz. dark rum
½ cup apple juice
slice of lemon

You can't resist repeating
this delicious temptation.

PARADISE PUNCH

Shake over crushed ice:
1¼ oz. light rum
Soda water — lime juice.
Apple juice..
Determine ~~amounts~~ for one or
more drinks.

Serve in tall frosted glass
with fresh mint garnish.

Apples stimulate the functions of the lungs, kidneys and liver. An apple before bedtime is said to induce sound restful sleep. (There is conflicting comment on the latter).

GRANNY SMITH SOUP

2 Granny Smith apples
1 pkg. frozen spinach
1 small onion — 2 T. butter
3 cups stock (chicken is best)
1½ cups milk - ¼ tsp. nutmeg
grated rind 1 lemon - Season s/p

Pare, core and quarter apples. Chop peeled onion. Combine in saucepan with butter and cook 10-12 mins. Add stock and spinach and heat at low temperature, adding spices. In about 20 minutes turn to a lower heat for about 10 minutes. Add milk and lemon and mix well. Bring to a quick boil, cover and stand aside about 5 minutes before serving.

APPLE DUMPLINGS with HAM

Soak 2 cups dried sweet apples
in water overnight. Simmer a
3 lb. ham butt for several hours.
Combine with apples and add
½ cup brown sugar.
Dumplings:
1 beaten egg mixed with
1 cup sifted flour, ¾ tsp.
baking soda, 1¼ tsp. cream
of tartar and dash of salt.
Add 2 Tablespoons butter and
⅓-½ cup milk. Mix well.

Drop batter into bubbling ham and
apples. Secure lid well.
Steam about 15 minutes without
uncovering.

> Coleridge holds that a man
> cannot have a pure mind who
> refuses apple dumplings.
>   Charles Lamb
>   Grace Before Meat

"APPLE"-tizing Soup

½ cup chopped peeled apple
½ cup finely chopped carrots
¼ cup chopped onion
1 cup minced cooked ham
¼ cup unsalted butter
¼ cup flour — 2 cups milk
2 cups apple juice
½ lb. grated sharp Cheddar cheese
Ground pepper — Apple slices

Combine first five ingredients over medium heat about 5 minutes. Add flour and blend until smooth. Add juice and milk. Mixture will look curdled at first but cook until boiling, then add cheese and lower to medium heat. Season. Serve hot in mugs or bowls. Garnish spoonful sour cream topped with a thin slice of apple.

Unlike Maple Syrup that is best from old trees, the finest apples come from young orchards.

ADAM'S FALL

Combine hot cider with dark rum — (1¼ oz. per serving of rum). Spice cider and stand aside several hours before mixing — adding cloves, lemon rind and sticks of cinnamon.

I've heard that Eve liked this recipe too!

October Chutney

Combine and cook until thickened:
2 qts. assorted sliced apples
1½ qts. small sliced green tomatoes
1 qt. small sliced onions
¾ qt. herbal vinegar* (tarragon)
1½ c. light brown sugar
1 tsp. ginger — ½ tsp. cinnamon
Dash of salt

*Wine vinegar or basil vinegar
is also good in this recipe.

"Simplicité de la cuisine
ne doit pas exclure la
qualité."

BIG APPLE SOUP

¾ c. apple juice
¾ c. dry white house wine
½ c. sugar
Pinch nutmeg and ginger
1½ c. chopped purple plums
1 large apple, grated

Combine ½ c. wine, apple juice and spices. Bring to a boil. Add plums and boil until they are soft, about 15 minutes. Strain. Stir in ½ c. sugar. Stand aside until cool. Now add ½ c. whipped cream and 3 tsp. fresh lemon juice and the rest of the wine. Chill and serve, topping with grated apple.

Budding and grafting were practised
before the Christian era. When grafting, each part united continues to
function normally but each maintains
its individual characteristics in the
fruit.

APPLE SOUP WISCONSIN

1 cup diced apple
1 cup dried apricots
1 cup chopped pitted prunes
¾ cup sultana raisins
¼ cup white sugar
½ lemon, thinly sliced
3 Tablespoon quick-cooking tapioca
6 cups water
1 teaspoon apple-pie mixed spice

Combine all except the apples
in a large pot. Mix well and
slowly bring to boil. Add
apples after about 10 minutes
and boil gently until apples
are tender. Be sure to cover
when removed from heat. Do
not serve hot — best served
warm or cold.

The Northern Spy was first named at an UpState New York farm in 1845.

OHIO CHUTNEY

Combine:
1 qt. chopped cooking apples
1 cup Mandarin oranges, in
      sections, rind and all
1 qt. ripe tomatoes. (Dip in hot
   water, remove skins, chop)
1 qt. small sliced onions
2 large chopped garlic cloves
1 cup chopped sultana raisins
Mix well, then add:
1½ T. gr. cloves — 1 T. salt
2 cups wine vinegar. Boil
gently, then simmer about
80 minutes, being careful not to
scorch.
Mix in 2 more cups vinegar
and 2 lbs. light brown sugar.
Cook gently 20 minutes. Spoon
into wide-mouthed jelly jars
and cover immediately.

SANTA FE SLAW

Combine in blender:
½ cup dairy sour cream
2 Tablespoons milk
1-2 teaspoons creamed horseradish
Dash salt and white pepper.
Set aside.

Peel and shred about 6 small
beets to make 3 cups. Combine
with 2 medium tart apples,
shredded. Add the dressing and
toss. Chill in refrigerator several
hours before serving. (Beets should
be cooked and cooled).

Serve on individual plates,
Topping each with slivered
blanched almonds and chopped
parsley.

"Good food is always a
trouble and its preparation
should be regarded as a
labour of love."
                    Elizabeth David

110

According to legend, when Venus bribed Paris to award her the golden apple, as being "the most beautiful", the vengeance of the other two contestants brought about the Trojan War.

APPLE VINEGAR

Mix together 5 pints cider with 1 pint cider vinegar. Cover and store. In about 8 weeks, skim the top, then strain into bottles.

Save colored wine and liqueur bottles and give apple vinegar to friends and visitors.

"Now the squeez'd press foams with our apple hoards."   1732

111

"A word fitly spoken is like apples of gold, in pictures of silver." Proverbs

WISCONSIN PUDDING

6 large apples, stewed
Beat 6 eggs and add ½ cup sugar.
When blended, add stewed apples,
¾ cup soft butter, juice and grated
rind of 1 lemon and dash of salt.

Pound 3 hard biscuits and break
into small pieces - not crumbs.
Fold into first mixture and add
1 cup heavy cream.

Using a greased pudding dish,
bake about a half hour at 300°.
This pudding can be served either
hot or cold.

Each seed produces a different
apple reflecting happenings at
some remote period in the life
of the species.

112

APPLE ALEXANDER

Mix equal parts of:
  Apple juice
  creme de cacao
  brandy
  heavy cream

Shake well with crushed ice.

HALIFAX TEMPTATIONS

(1) Combine apple juice with equal parts of dark rum and Cointreau. Guaranteed to give a punch!

(2) Combine apple juice with gin or vodka and Collins mix, or tonic water with slices of lemon. A summer refresher.

ACADIAN FLAN

Begin with a short crust pastry.
Sift together 2 cups plain flour
and dash of salt. Work with
fingertips while adding 8 T.
butter, 1 egg and 1/4 cup cold
water.
Knead lightly until smooth.
Wrap in foil and cool until
ready to use, or 30 minutes.
Use an 8" flan ring.

Peel, core and chunk 2 lbs.
apples. Combine these in a
saucepan with 1/2 cup white
wine, rind of half a large
lemon, 4 T. butter and 1/4 cup
sugar. Simmer gently,
covered, and when apples are
tender, remove lemon rind
and set pan aside.

(Continued)

114

(Cont'd.)

Pureé the apples and place them in an unbaked shell. Now peel and core 4 medium tart apples, slice thinly and arrange them over the pureé, making your own design. Sprinkle with ½ cup sugar and bake at 375°; for about ½ hour.

Heat apricot jam, about 3 Table-spoons, and mix with 1 Table-spoon lemon juice. With brush, glaze hot flan with the apricot lemon mixture. Serve with a heaping bowl of whipped cream.

Variation: Omit top layer of tart apples and substitute very thin slices of 4 oranges, poaching them first in ½ c. sugar and ½ cup of water. Glaze with apricot jam, melted.

SWEET POTATO and APPLE

6 sweet potatoes — 3 apples
2 T. melted butter — 1/4 cup rum
1/2 c. orange juice — 1/4 tsp. all spice
1/4 c. dark brown sugar

Boil or steam the potatoes until
tender. Skin, then cut lengthwise
into slices. Peel and core the
apples and slice in rings.
Butter an oblong baking dish
and alternate layers of potato
and apple slices until dish is
filled. Pour over it the orange
juice, sugar, spices, rum and
butter.
Bake in preheated oven 350° for
30 minutes. The top should be
brown and shiny and the liquid
absorbed.

Apples — "hard and dry, sweet
and juicy, green, yellow or red,
the (ANNAPOLIS) Valley has
produced them all."

Barbecued Apples

Preheat oven to 350°

Cut 4 apples in half and core. Place in a shallow pan with cut sides up. Cover each one with

1 Tablespoon Catchup
1 " brown sugar

Dot each one with butter Add about ¼" hot water. Bake 30 minutes Serve hot. Spoon over the roast or chops — if any liquid remains.

In the 18th century and into the 19th, nearly every rural home in Nova Scotia and New England and the U.S. mid-west had an apple paring machine clamped to the kitchen table and operated with a crank. The pared apples were quartered by hand with a knife and cores removed.

CURRIED HAM with APPLE

1 10 oz. can cream of mushroom soup
2 lbs. cubed cooked ham
1 large apple, cored and chopped
2 tsp. curry powder
3 small green onions (slice entire stalk)
1 cup sour cream - dash of cayenne

Add ham and seasonings to soup. When hot add sour cream, apple and onions. Do not burn.

Serve over toast or fill hard rolls and cover with sauce.

Charred remains of Apple trees were found in the prehistoric lake dwellings of Switzerland.

APPLES and ROSES

In an unbaked crust, layer sliced apples mixed with confectioner's sugar and red rose petals. Dot with butter and ½ teaspoon all spice. Top with crust and bake 45-50 minutes at 350°.
This is an early-settler recipe.

GRATED APPLE and CABBAGE

3 apples, grated
1 small red cabbage, grated
1 large onion, minced - 2 T. butter
1/3 cup Tarragon (or wine) Vinegar
1/3 cup Water - 2 T. sugar
2 tsp. each salt and pepper

Add cabbage to pan of boiling
water and cook 1 minute. Drain.
Saute onion and apples in butter
for about 3 minutes. Make
alternate layers of the cabbage
and onion/apple mixture in a
buttered casserole, sprinkling
with sugar, salt, pepper, vinegar
and water. Cover and cook
about 1 hour at 325°.

This recipe encourages the
cook to be creative. The
number of apples, etc. can
vary with the occasion.

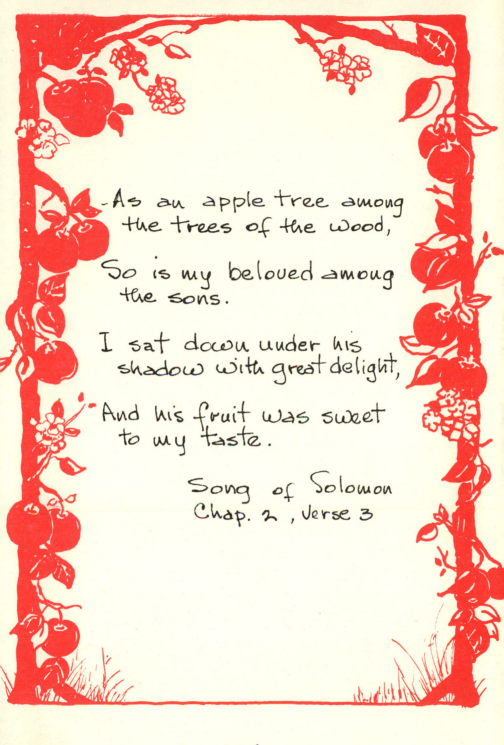

-As an apple tree among
the trees of the wood,

So is my beloved among
the sons.

I sat down under his
shadow with great delight,

And his fruit was sweet
to my taste.

Song of Solomon
Chap. 2 , Verse 3

SCALLOPED APPLES

Combine:
Soft bread crumbs to cover bottom of baking dish and ¼ cup butter. Slice apples to nearly fill dish. Mix into apples 2 T. sugar, dash of nutmeg, cinnamon and salt, and 1 T. each grated lemon rind and juice. Spread soft bread crumbs on top. Bake at 350° for about 40 minutes. Do not burn! Serve with hot lemon sauce

APPLE RINGS

Wash and core 5 apples. Slice at least ¼" thick. Arrange on foil on broiler pan. Make mixture of butter and lemon juice and brush liberally. Carefully turn the slices and repeat, after about 4 minutes under broiler. Sprinkle with 1 Tablespoon sugar mixed with ¼ teaspoon cinnamon. Broil 2-3 minutes longer.

SAUCY BEANS

2 cans Boston-style oven
    baked beans
2 cups natural applesauce
6-8 all-beef hot dogs, split
    if desired.

Place beans in a bean crock
or casserole dish. Arrange
hot dogs on the top and
cover with the applesauce.
Bake at 350° about 45 minutes,
until bubbling hot.
Serves 4-6.

APPLE BUTTER

Whip together apple sauce and butter. Serve in a crock with muffins or dark sweet breads as part of salad bar or bread board.

The first commercial apple orchards in Wisconsin were planted between 1830 and 1850.

BERWICK APPLE BROIL

Place slice of ham on light rye bread. Cover with apple slices and a slice of Cheddar Cheese. Broil. Serve with apple butter.

By the mid 1800's, apple orchards were a part of every farm where land was settled in Canada and in the U.S.A.

BLACKBERRY-APPLE PUDDING

For several years, before I found Cranberrie Cottage, I had a summer place with 30 acres looking over the water, in Clementsport, N.S. I shall never forget the times spent there.

The hill beyond the house was cleared and at the top, along the lot line, I would dig for hours retrieving treasures from the past. My favourite is a cobalt blue whale oil lamp with big hearts around the bowl. It sits in a window at Cranberrie Cottage. The base has been mended because one summer I found a piece of the cobalt blue and for some reason I kept it; The following summer I found the rest of the lamp.

Alongside the house the land was densely wooded with wild cherry, ash and birch-and alders. Underfoot and fiercely guarding the trees were masses of blackberries. Gradually the land sloped upward with wild apple trees and birch, giving way finally to spruce surrounded by a carpet of red gold chanterelles. At the top of the hill it was a magic world of silver stumps, huge maples, beech and aspens — and blackberries growing around gnarled broken apple trees. I loved that place and knew every tree by heart.

The apples were beautiful to look at but bitter to taste. The blackberries were royal - the size of a walnut — jet black and brimming over with blackberry sweetness. One day I found an old lilac bush and several wild gooseberry bushes. I tried to visualize the early French Acadians who were deeded that land so long ago, and who first cultivated the apple trees in Nova Scotia.

Somewhere I have a scribbler
of blackberry recipes, gathered
or invented during those Clementsport summers. Here is one of my
favourites.

BLACKBERRY-APPLE PUDDING

Make your favourite pastry, but
sometime try a suet crust.

Grease a 6" mold and line it
with a third of the dough. Slice
about 5 apples and mix with
2 cups blackberries, ½ cup
sugar and ¼ cup water. Secure
top crust and cover with wax
paper. Steam about 2½-3 hours.
Serve with whipped cream.
(Fruit amounts can be adjusted
to size, and sugar to taste).

A variation is to roll dough
about 8" long and ½" thick. Cover
with fruit and roll up. Moisten
edges well. Bake on greased
sheet about 1 hour at 400°.

127

APPLE-TURNIP COMBINATION

1 small turnip, about size of grapefruit
3 slices bacon — 1/2 c. sour cream
1 large chopped apple — Thyme
1 Tablespoon butter

Cut up the turnip and bacon, add
a scant amount of water. Simmer,
then boil. Let stand about
10 minutes, then drain. Beat
well, adding half of the sour
cream. Fold in the butter, beat
again and add the remainder
of the sour cream.

Cook chopped unpeeled apple
in separate saucepan, using
scant amount of water. When
tender, combine the apple
with the turnip. Season to
taste.

Serve immediately, or place
in casserole dish to heat longer
in oven or to serve later.

APPLE TARTLETS

Prepare pastry crust as if for a 9" - 2 crust pie, to which is added 1/4 cup grated cheddar cheese. Roll out on floured board and cut into 4" squares.

Fill each square with a mixture of: 2 cups diced dried apples that had soaked about an hour in 1 1/2 cups hot water and then cooked until tender, 1/2 cups light brown sugar, 1/2 cup broken nut meats and a dash of salt.

Moisten edges of squares and bring together. Bake about 20-25 minutes at 400°.

CANADA'S APPLE-GROWING AREAS
There are five main areas in Canada where the climate and soil conditions are ideal for producing top-quality apples. These include the Annapolis Valley in Nova Scotia; the St. John River Valley in New Brunswick; the southern section of Quebec; most of the counties in the St. Lawrence Valley and around the lower Great Lakes in southern Ontario; and the Okanagan Valley in British Columbia.

COCONUT-APPLE STRUDEL

1½ Tbsp. quick-cooking tapioca
½ c. sugar — ⅛ tsp. salt
¾ tsp. cinnamon — ¼ tsp. nutmeg
5 c. peeled sliced apples
1 Tbsp. lemon juice
Pastry for 1-crust pie
½ c. flaked coconut

Combine first 7 ingredients. Mix well. Line 9-inch pan with pastry. Fill with apple mixture. Bake at 425° for 25 minutes or until apples are tender.
Sprinkle crumb topping over the apples and top with coconut. Bake another 10 minutes.

Topping:
Combine ⅓ c. brown sugar, ⅓ c. fine graham cracker crumbs, and ¼ c. soft butter. Mix well until crumbs are size of peas.

130

COOKIE GLAZE

1-½ cup Confectioner's sugar
1 Tablespoon butter
2-½ Tablespoons cream (milk)
Vanilla   — Pinch of salt

Combine and mix well. Glaze
cookies with brush while
cookies are hot.

APPLE BLOSSOM SHAKE

1 qt. apple juice, chilled
1 pt. vanilla ice cream, softened
2 T. red currant jelly

Blend, or use mixer, serve
frothy. Sprinkle each glass
with nutmeg.

Variation — omit jelly and add
1- 8¾ oz. can crushed pineapple

ORIENT PORK with APPLE

3 cups chopped apples
1 cup slivered green pepper
2 cups lean pork in small pieces
3½ T. Sunflower oil - 3 onions
1½ c. hot water
Canned bean sprouts (2 cups)
2½ cups sliced celery
3 T. Soy sauce - 2½ T. cornstarch
4 T. cold water - salt

Lightly brown pork with onion and green pepper in oil. Simmer in the bean sprout liquid mixed with 1½ cup water about 30 minutes. Combine apples with celery, soy sauce and a dash of salt. Add to first mixture. Cook about 20 minutes.

Dissolve cornstarch in cold water. Blend into mixture. Finally, add the bean sprouts. Serve hot, seasoning with Soy sauce, over rice.

The first apple-wife was Pomona.
1599

132

Roast Chicken with Apple

Brown chicken well.
An average fowl is well browned
about 20 minutes at 450° on each
side. Allow to cool slightly.
Arrange a layer of cored halved
apples on bottom of roasting
pan and place bird on them.
Season apples to taste.
When about ½ hour to being
done, place thick slices of
Apple (4 to an apple) around
the chicken. Sprinkle over
them about ½ cup brandy
mixed with ¼ cup "half and
half" cream.

Ice Cream Cider Sauce

Combine 1/2 cup brown sugar,
1 1/2 tablespoons cornstarch
and 1/2 teaspoon each nutmeg
and cinnamon.
Stir in 2 cups apple cider.
Cook slowly, stirring constantly, until thickened.
Add 2 Tablespoons butter.
Serve hot over ice cream,
pound cake or Upside-Down
cake.

Apples à la Greque

Prepare spinach for salad. Add
pinch of nutmeg and cinnamon
to oil and vinegar dressing
base. Toss spinach, sliced
firm, unpared apples, small
chunks feta cheese with the
dressing. Serve with Greek
entreés, or as part of a
salad bar buffet.

BLACK APPLE JELLY

Cook equal amounts blackberries
and apples, in separate pots, in
just enough water to cover.
When tender, strain through
two jelly bags.
Mix the blackberry and apple
juice and measure the liquid.
Bring to a boil. Add 1½ cup
sugar for every cup of liquid.
Boil until set test. Stand
aside about 20 minutes, then
ladle into hot dry glasses.

YAMS and SPYS

(Do not peel the yams.) Boil
about 6 yams until barely
tender. Peel and slice, not too
thin. Peel, core and slice 4
large Spys.
Layer yams and apples in a
buttered baking dish. Sprinkle
each layer with brown sugar,
butter and nutmeg. Top with
about 1/2 cup apple cider and
bake 40-50 minutes or until
apples are tender.
Great with roast Goose!

APPLE FUNDY

Combine 1/2 cup light brown sugar with
salt to taste, and 4 beaten egg yolks.
Add grated rind of 1 lemon and 2
cups Applesauce. Mix thoroughly.
Beat egg whites. When stiff, fold into
first mixture. Heap into buttered
baking dish. Set dish in hot water
and bake until soufflé is set
(350°) and golden.   Serve at once.

GRANVILLE COFFEE CAKE

Combine and bring to a boil, 1 cup each sugar and water with about 3 cloves. Add 3 tart sliced apples and simmer until tender. Cool, remove apples and drain. (Remove cloves)

Knead about half recipe of plain bread dough on floured board, covering a jelly roll pan. Top with apples. Spread over them a mixture of 1 beaten egg, 2 Tablespoons each of butter and light brown sugar. Wrap the dough around the filling. Place in a warm room until it has tripled in size. Twist to form a circle, stick with blanched almonds and candied citron. Bake 10 mins. at 450° and 25 mins. at 350°. Cool on rack. Sprinkle with Confectioner's sugar.

AN ANCIENT TEMPTATION

Boil unpared apples, then puree.
Combine with "almond milk" (this
is an emulsion of water and
sweet blanched almonds) and
liquid honey, adding bread
crumbs, saffron and salt.
Boil gently "and loke that thou
stir it well, and serve it forth."

This 15th century recipe depends
for its effectiveness on the good
culinary sense - and courage
and imagination of the cook.
Even today, the good cook tends
to modify most recipes.

138

In American folklore, Johnny Appleseed is the archetype of "endurance that was voluntary, and of action that was creative and not sanguinary."

ROASTED TIPSY PORK CHOPS

Cover each chop liberally with this mixture:
Sauté a large onion, chopped fine, in butter, until tender. Stir in about 2 medium grated apples. In about 3 minutes add 1 T. flour, ½ cup cider and salt and pepper to taste. Continue to heat and stir for about 20 minutes.

*One of the symbols of Aphrodite,
Goddess of Love, was an apple.*

A Dutch Treat
(Apples and Red Cabbage)

Using a heavy casserole, melt
about 1 Tablespoon butter. Add
2 medium onions sliced about ¼"
thick, 3 large carrots sliced same
thickness, and 6 strips of bacon.
Cook about 8 minutes.
Remove dish from heat and add
4 large apples cut into slices,
1 clove minced garlic and a 2-2½
pound red cabbage, sliced about
½" thick.
Season to taste with salt and
pepper, adding 2 bay leaves,
2 whole cloves, 3 Tablespoons
port and 2 Tablespoons red
wine vinegar.
Cover with lid or foil and bake
at 325° for 2 hours or until
tender.

Apples are New York State's most important fruit crop with an annual production of approximately 26 million bushel and increasing due to new plantings coming into production.

EDUCATED APPLE SOUP

I first made this soup when a graduate student at Cornell. My neighbor was a Pomology major and he would bring me "educated apples" from the Cornell orchards!

4 large apples - 2½ c. water
1 tsp. grated ginger root - 2 T. sugar
2 T. white bread crumbs - salt
Rind and juice of 1 orange
2 T. red currant jelly - ½ tsp. cinnamon
1⅔ c. light fruity wine

Combine sliced apples, bread, orange rind and spices with water. Cook 10 minutes. Add juice and jelly and sugar. Stir well. Bring to boil, then cool and pureé. Add salt and wine. Chill well before serving.

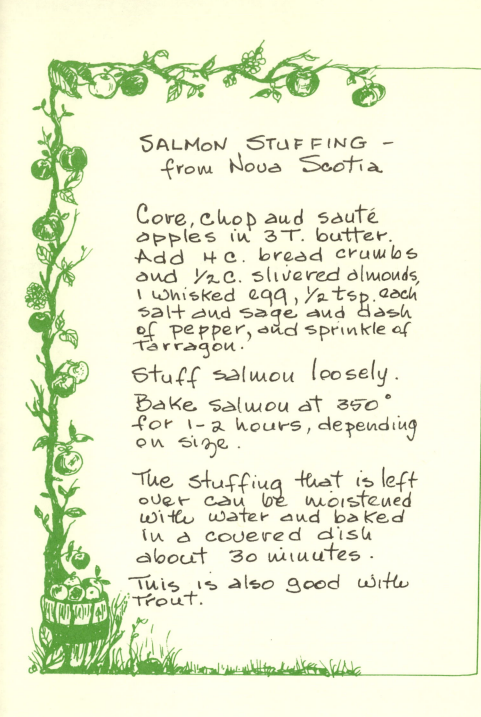

SALMON STUFFING – from Nova Scotia

Core, chop and sauté apples in 3 T. butter. Add 4 c. bread crumbs and ½ c. slivered almonds, 1 whisked egg, ½ tsp. each salt and sage and dash of pepper, and sprinkle of tarragon.

Stuff salmon loosely.

Bake salmon at 350° for 1-2 hours, depending on size.

The stuffing that is left over can be moistened with water and baked in a covered dish about 30 minutes.

This is also good with trout.

Apples go well with cabbage-
whether cooked or raw, green
or red, or as sauerkraut.

Sometimes there is only a
slight variation between recipes
and the good cook can add
her/his own touch. I could
not resist including several
versions of Apples cooked or
served with cabbage.

Bucks County Cabbage

4 apples - 2 lbs. red cabbage
2 onions - 2 c. water
1/4 c. butter - 2 tsp. each salt/pepper
1/2 tsp. nutmeg - 3 T. cider vinegar
Juice of 1 large lemon

Chop onions and saute in butter.
Add spices and cook until tender.
Stir in shredded cabbage with
water and vinegar. Cook, covered,
about a half hour. Slice
apples and cook until tender,
about 25 minutes. When cool,
stir in lemon juice. Serve.

OLD FASHIONED APPLESAUCE

6 sliced cooking apples, boiled until tender in about 6 Tablespoons water. Add 1/4 cup sugar, 1/4 each tbsp. salt and nutmeg to 1/4 cup (2 ozs) butter. Combine gently to mashed apples. Cool and serve.

"Thy breath is like the streame of apple-pyes."

ARCADIA, 1590

'KRAUT with APPLES

This recipe uses canned 'Kraut. Heat contents of a 2-lb. can, in top of double-boiler, for about 15 minutes.
Combine 3 sliced apples with 6 strips chopped bacon and sauté until the bacon is almost cooked. Add an onion, minced, and cook 1-2 minutes. Add the warmed 'Kraut and heat well.

This dish could be cooked in the oven – Polish Sausage could be substituted for the bacon.

144

Fill the cool-room with home-
made applesauce, when the
ground is covered with windfalls.

San Francisco Sandwich

2 cups apple sauce, heated
16 strips lean bacon, crisp
8 slices pasteurized cheese
8 slices rye bread

Toast bread on one side.
Place slice of cheese on the
untoasted side. Broil. When
cheese melts, top with hot
applesauce and crisp slices
of bacon. Serve immediately.

145

ACADIAN DELIGHT
(Soufflé aux pommes)

1 cup applesauce - 2 egg yolks
4 T. apricot jam - 2 egg whites
1/4 c. sugar - slivered almonds

Combine applesauce, jam and
sugar and cook over medium
heat until mixture is thick.
Remove from heat and whisk in
the egg yolks.
Beat egg whites until stiff, then
gently fold into the warm mixture.
Now quickly but gently fold in
about 1/2 cup slivered almonds.

Pour into baking/serving dish
that is buttered and sugared.
Bake in moderate oven (325°)
about 20 minutes. Serve at once.

(The first part of recipe can be
prepared early. Just before
dinner add egg whites and cook
during dinner. Serve with or
without whipped cream.)

146

FRUIT DIP

Blend together with a fork, about 2 cups crumbled blue cheese, grated rind of 1 large orange and sour cream, enough to make a smooth creamy dip. Chill well. To serve, stand at room temperature about 25 minutes, and surround with segments of orange, slices of un-peeled pear (4) and 2 sliced red and 2 sliced green apples.

147

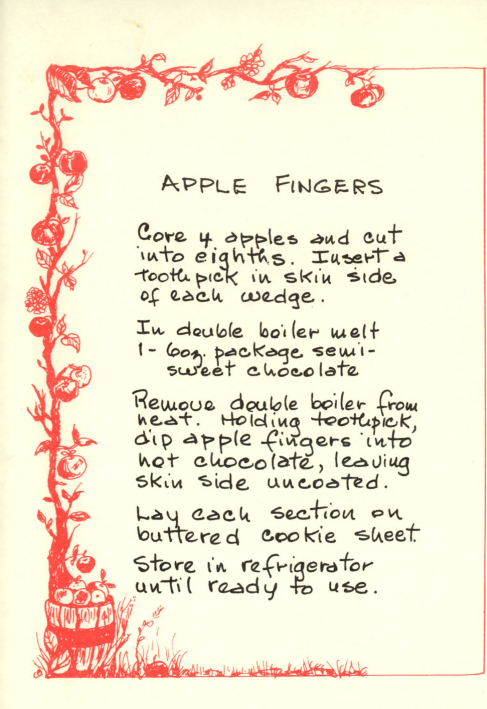

APPLE FINGERS

Core 4 apples and cut into eighths. Insert a toothpick in skin side of each wedge.

In double boiler melt 1- 6oz. package semi-sweet chocolate

Remove double boiler from heat. Holding toothpick, dip apple fingers into hot chocolate, leaving skin side uncoated.

Lay each section on buttered cookie sheet.

Store in refrigerator until ready to use.

The duration of time of prime
quality for an apple is often no
more than a day, especially for
summer apples.

ANN ARBOR APPLE PIE

Melt 28 vanilla caramels in
about 2 Tablespoons water.
Stir until smooth.
Layer 4 cups sliced pared
apples with the caramel
sauce, in an unbaked pie
shell.
Combine
   3/4 cup all-purpose flour
   1/3 cup sugar
   1/2 tsp. cinnamon.
Cut in 1/3 cup butter (margarine)
until pea-sized crumbs. Stir
in 1/2 cup broken slivered almonds.
Sprinkle over apple mixture.
Bake about 1 hour at 375° or
until apples are tender.

The "Wealthy" apple originated
in Minnesota. Parentage unknown.

149

SHRUB with RASPBERRY and CIDER

2 cups cider — ½ cup lime juice
1 cup raspberry syrup –
3 cups gingerale
Ginger root, grated – about 2 T.
Mix well. Chill. (10-12 cups)

There were no native apple
trees in North America. The
early Acadians brought with
them the skill of grafting.

150

To make an "appillmose", "tak
appelles and sethe them and
lett them kelle, then fret them
throughe an heryn syff."

Noble Book Cookery
1450

APPLE TARTS

2½ c. sliced apples
4 oz. shredded coconut
½ cup currants (or dried blueberries)
1 cup sugar - Juice and rind 1 lemon
1 egg   - 2 T. melted butter
Flaky pastry

Quarter apples and combine with
all except egg and butter. When
well mixed, beat egg, add butter,
and fold into mixture.
Roll out pastry in 4" squares,
⅛" thick. Spoon some of the
mixture on each square, wet
edges with milk and fold over
to make a triangle. Tine edges.
Bake in hot oven about 25-30
minutes. Serve warm.

151

An apple-eating person is one
easily tempted.
"Foolish, credulous and apple-
eating women will believe them."
1620

PORK SAUCE

Sauté about 6 small green onions
in butter for about 5 minutes,
using a deep skillet. Gradually
stir in ¾ cup apple cider (or juice)
and 1 can consommé. Boil gently
about a half hour.
Peel 2 large firm apples, cut
into small chunks, add to the
mixture and cook gently for
5 minutes. Season to taste.
Serve hot over chops or
steaks.

When Geo. Washington ran in the
legislature in 1758 his agent
doled out beer, wine, apple cider
or rum — to every voter.

 Make "juicy" ice cubes with apple juice garnished
with apple chunks. Or the night before, make an
apple juice ice mold for your favorite punch
recipe.

153

CRANBERRIE COTTAGE APPLES
(Pommes à la chez-soi)

4 cooking apples
2 cups water - 1 cup sugar
1/4 cup candied fruits
Pastry Custard
3/4 cup cooky crumbs
1/4 cup melted butter

Combine water and sugar and bring to a boil. Pare, core and halve the apples, add to syrup and simmer until barely tender. Place apples, rounded side down, in shallow casserole. Place candied fruits in each centre, then cover with the custard which has been made while apples are simmering. Cover each apple with cooky crumbs and dot with melted butter. Bake in hot oven (400°) until browned.

Pastry Custard ————>

154

PASTRY CUSTARD (Crème Patisserie)

This custard is intended as a filling for pies or tarts. It is ideal to serve with lady fingers or, as in this recipe, as a special dessert.

Beat 4 egg yolks with ¾ cup sugar - about 3 minutes. Gradually add 2 cups milk (scalded or cold).
Stir and heat slowly but do not boil. (I use a wooden spoon for best results). Remember, the custard should not boil. Remove from heat. Add 1 Tablespoon Rum. Serve hot or cold.

Apple pies and apple fritters,
Apple cores to feed the critters.

Johnny Appleseed
1774 - 1855

155

APPLE MERINGUE PIE

6-8 tart apples, sliced
Mix apples with ½ cup sugar
and ½ teaspoon grated lemon
rind and ¼ teaspoon nutmeg.
Heap into unbaked shell and
cook at 375° until apples are
tender. Do not overcook.
When done, set pie aside to
cool, about 2 hours.
Make a meringue with whites of
3 eggs and ½ tsp. almond extract
and 3 T. Confectioner's sugar.
Heap atop apple mixture and
bake at 350° about 10 minutes,
or until golden brown.

There is on-going tremendous
growth in the apple industry
in Japan.

156

An "apple peeling frolic" was a
social avent among the early
settlers.

SUMMER SPECIAL

4 cups chopped green apples
4 cups chopped young rhubarb
1 cup crushed pineapple, drained
1 cup seedless raisins
Grated rind and juice of 1 small
orange and lemon.
4½ cups white sugar - dash of salt.
½ tbsp. ea. nutmeg, cloves, all spice

Mix all ingredients together, adding
the pineapple juice. Stand aside
all night. Heat, simmer until thick
but watch that it does not stick
nor burn. Ladle into hot jars.

"Huskings and apple-parings
had not gone out of fashion."
                                    1879

157

BAKED TAPIOCA APPLES

Soak about ¾ cup tapioca an hour in water. Drain and cook in double-boiler with 2½ cups water. Butter a serving dish (casserole) and place in it 8 firm cored apples, filled with mixture of cranberry sauce and maple syrup. Top with Tapioca and bake at 350° until apples are tender. Serve with cream.

Thousands of seedlings are grown from pips before one quality fruit appears.

VARIATIONS on APPLE FILLING

1. Combine ¾ c. chopped cranberries, ½ c. sugar, 3 T. chopped nuts and 1 T. honey.

2. Combine ¼ c. seedless raisins, ¼ c. slivered blanched almonds and 1½ T. honey

The red astrachan came from Russia.

Left-over squeezed apples from the cider press is called Pomace. It is used to add to the feed of beef cattle.

SWEET and SOUR APPLES

2 tart unpeeled apples, quartered
1 medium red cabbage, shredded
1 medium onion, sliced in rings
5 strips bacon, crisp and in bits
1 cup water - 1/4 cup cider vinegar
1/2 cup red table wine - 1 T. sugar

Fry bacon until crisp. Drain and saute onion in the bacon fat. Add cabbage, vinegar, wine and water. Season with salt and pepper. Cook about 15 minutes, then add the quartered apples. (Water or apple juice can be substituted for wine — but it is best with wine). Cook slowly until tender.

Cooking is like love, it should be entered into with abandon or not at all.
                    Harriet Van Horne

159

Boston Salad

Cook ½ pound bacon until crisp.
Drain and break into small pieces.
Tear 1 head lettuce into bite-
sized pieces. Quarter and core
3 apples (CORTLAND, DELICIOUS
and GRANNY SMITH). Do not peel.
Slice and drop each one into
garlic oil. Stir in 2 tsp. lemon
juice. Add
  ½ tsp. black pepper, salt,
  1 bunch scallions, sliced
  1 egg – 1 cup croutons

Toss thoroughly until egg well
mixed.

Garlic Vegetable Oil: drop garlic
cloves (2-3, peeled and mashed)
into ⅔ cup vegetable oil. Leave
for several hours or a day before
using.

"The children's garden is in apple-
pie order."   SCOTT, 1813

APPLE AND MEAT BALLS

Mix together about a cup of minced veal, 2 cups minced pork and a Tablespoon of fresh sage, chopped fine. To this mixture add about 4 apples, peeled, cored and roughly grated, 2 Tablespoons fine bread crumbs and salt and pepper to taste. Mix well.

Roll mixture into tiny balls, flour lightly. Cook in chafing dish until browned on both sides and cooked through. Do not overcook — about 12-15 minutes.

X=Annapolis Valley

CRANBERRIE COTTAGE CAKE

Grease and lightly flour a 10"
tube or bundt pan and preheat
oven to 350°
Peel, core and shred 5 good-
sized apples. Toss these with
5 Tablespoons sugar and 2 Tablespoons cinnamon. Set aside.
In a large bowl combine:
  3 cups unsifted flour
  2½ cups sugar - ½ tsp. salt
  4 eggs - 1 cup saffron oil
  1 tsp. vanilla - ⅓ c. apple juice
  1½ tsp. each baking powder and soda

If you prefer to use an electric
mixer, blend at low speed for
1 minute. Scrape sides of
bowl, increase to medium
speed for another 3 minutes.

Fill prepared bundt pan, starting and ending with a layer
of batter and alternating with
an apple layer.   (Continued)

(Con'd)
This should make a total
of 3 batter and 2 apple layers.

Bake 1½ - 1¾ hours at 350°.
Cool about 10-15 minutes on
a rack.

Invert cake and remove from
bundt. Glaze with a mixture
of Confectioner's sugar, butter,
vanilla and apple juice until
smooth — while cake is warm.

Glaze:
1½ c. Confectioner's Sugar
2 Tablespoons butter
1½ teaspoons apple juice
½ teaspoon vanilla extract

The three most popular
apples grown in No. America
are the McIntosh, Cortland
and Delicious.

163

An English Apple Pie

Make your favourite pastry adding about ¼ cup grated cheddar cheese - OR - make a rich cheese pastry by mixing together:

   ¾ c. sifted allpurpose flour
   ½ c. butter - ½ c. grated cheddar
   1 beaten egg yolk - 2 tsp. water
   ⅛ tsp. each mustard and salt

Filling:

   Enough sliced apples to fill a 9" pastry filled dish.
   In a skillet mix and heat: ¼ cup light brown sugar, ¼ cup butter and grated rind and juice of 1 lemon (or orange). Gently toss apples into the mixture. Heap into crust lined dish and top with crust, securing rims. Cook 30 minutes at about 400°.

Most of the best apples were said to be introduced into Britain by the fruiterer of Henry the Eighth.   (1813)

164

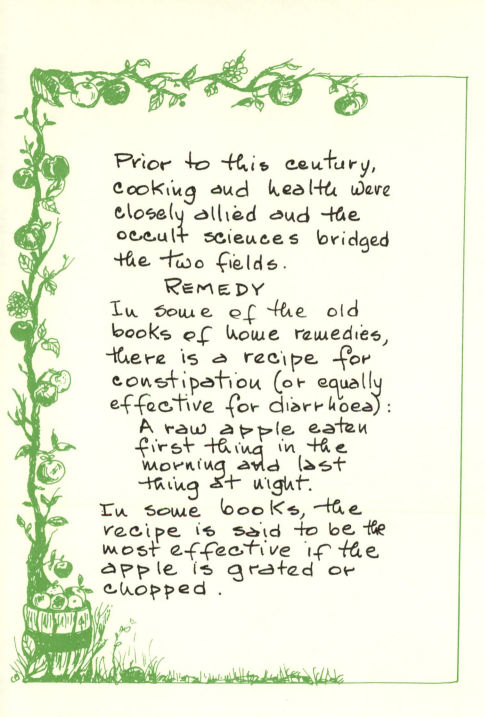

Prior to this century, cooking and health were closely allied and the occult sciences bridged the two fields.

REMEDY

In some of the old books of home remedies, there is a recipe for constipation (or equally effective for diarrhoea):

A raw apple eaten first thing in the morning and last thing at night.

In some books, the recipe is said to be the most effective if the apple is grated or chopped.

WALDORF SALAD

This recipe can be varied, amounts depending on number to be served.

1 large green apple - cold
1 large red apple - cold
1 cup celery, finely chopped
¾ cup broken walnuts
Juice of 1 small lemon
¼ cup mayonnaise
1 red apple, sliced, brushed with
   lemon juice.
Optional: raisins, green grapes

Dice the chilled apples. Cover with lemon juice. Combine with celery, nuts and mayonnaise. Serve on crisp lettuce. Garnish with red apple slices. Sprinkle grated lemon rind over each serving - not much - just a touch.

The original Delicious Apple tree (1872) came from Winterset, Iowa. Today there is a monument there to commemorate the event.

APPLE-FRITTER BATTER

Mix together:
1 cup flour   - 3 Tablespoon Icing
⅓ cup milk   -   Sugar (Confectioners)
1½ teaspoon baking powder - Salt
When well mixed, fold in one
well beaten egg.

ANNAPOLIS VALLEY, NOVA SCOTIA -
"a miracle of sweet smelling pink
and white blossoms - the promise of
plenty - greatest apple producing
country in the British Empire." 1937

APPLE PIE

5 medium tart apples - 1 T. lemon juice
⅓ c. light brown sugar - dash of salt
⅛ tsp. each nutmeg or cinnamon

Make your favourite pastry, adding
the grated rind of 1 small lemon.
Slice apples and fill bottom
crust. Add the mixture of sugar,
salt and spices. Sprinkle with
lemon juice. Top with crust.
Bake about 45 minutes at 350°.

167

STORE IN PLASTIC BAG OR HYDRATOR DRAWER to prevent absorbing other food flavors and to maintain proper humidity.

PEANUT BUTTER and APPLE SANDWICHES

½ cup peanut butter
2-3 Tablespoons honey

Combine and spread on 4 slices lightly toasted raisin bread. Core and slice 1 large apple and arrange slices on honey / peanut butter mixture. Top with lightly toasted raisin bread.

Cut diagonally twice and serve.

EDEN APPLES

Clean and core as many apples
as you need. Mix together
½ cup sugar and ¼ cup maple
syrup with ½ cup water for
6 apples. Put apples upright
in small saucepan and cover
with the syrup. (Add water if
needed). Cook until apples are
Tender. Remove carefully and cool.
Just before serving, fill each
apple with a mixture of crushed
almonds and marmalade _ or
your favourite filling. Serve
with whipped cream, or
plain cream, or sprinkle lightly
with Confectioner's sugar.

"Rough tasted appules are holesome when the stomacke is weake." 1449

APPLE TORTE

4 eggs, well beaten - dash salt
2/3 c. flour - 1½ c. sugar
1 tsp. baking powder - 1 tsp. vanilla
2 Apples (or enough to make 2 cups
         when peeled and chopped)
1 cup chopped pecans

Beat eggs at high speed for about 5 minutes until thick and light colored. Sift dry ingredients together and fold into egg mixture. Gently fold in apples, nuts and vanilla. Bake in a greased oblong pan (13 x 9½ x 2) at 350° for 40-45 minutes. Cool before removing from pan. Serves 12.

In the days of Pliny there were said to be 22 varieties of apples; in 1984 there were over 6000 varieties.

170

GRAND PRÉ CASSEROLE

2 cups cooked, chopped chicken
2 cups diced, unpared apples
½ cup sliced celery
¼ cup minced onion
1 can cream of chicken soup
1 tsp. sage - ½ tsp. salt
Dash of pepper

Using a 1½ quart baking dish,
combine chicken, apple, celery
and onion. Combine remaining
ingredients in a small bowl,
mixing well.
Combine mixtures and ladle
into baking dish.
Bake about 40 mins. at 350°,
or until hot and bubbly.
(6 servings, 166 calories each)

171

GOOSE STUFFING

There are many recipes for
goose dressing and most of
them use apples. I've heard
that the apple acts against
the greasiness of a cooked
goose.

① Prepare about 6 large apples
and chop - but not too fine.
Soak the apples in cheap
white rum at least 4 hours.
Just before stuffing the bird,
mix together about 6 sage
leaves, minced, and 1½ cups of
bread crumbs seasoned with
¼ teaspoon ground mace.

"names quite as inseparable
as goose and applesauce."
Miss Mitford, 1740

172

APPLE·MINT SAUCE

Whether you live in an apartment
or a house in the country, it is
a good culinary investment to
have a couple pots of mint.
At Cranberrie Cottage the mint
grows all around the back
steps and there is hardly
a day goes by that I don't bring
some branches into the house.
Mint is used in many ways
with Apples.

Gather fresh mint leaves.
Wash, dry and chop. Mix 2 T.
of white sugar and 8 T. of
cider vinegar to every 3 T. of
chopped mint leaves. Boil gently.
This sauce tastes best if
made a couple days before
using but keep in refrigerator.
Its a natural with roasted
lamb but use your imagination
for other wonderful ways.

SUNDAY UPSIDE-DOWN CAKE

Pare and core about 3 tart apples. Slice thin and simmer in 1 cup apple juice until barely tender - about 5 minutes. Drain but keep the apple juice.

Combine 2 Tablespoons hot juice with 1/3 cup butter and 1 cup packed brown sugar and put in a 13x9x2 inch pan. Set in 350° oven for 5 minutes, then remove.

Prepare 1 package spice cake mix, substituting apple juice for water.

Arrange apple slices and halved Maraschino cherries in the brown sugar mixture in pan. Sprinkle with 1/2 cup chopped walnuts. Pour batter into pan. Bake about 1 hour - 350°. Remove from oven, invert 1 minute.
(Continued)

174

(Cont'd)
Remove cake from pan.
Serve while warm, with
topping. This is a real temptation!

Topping:

Whip 1 cup heavy cream
until stiff, adding 1/4 cup
Confectioner's sugar,
1 teaspoon vanilla and
1/4 cup sliced almonds.

If Topping is to be placed
in a serving bowl, sprinkle
the almonds on top.

(Canned apples work well
with this recipe).

APPLE RELISH

6 chopped apples, 1 cup chunk pineapple (save the juice). Simmer apples in the juice, then add the pineapple. Spice to taste. Cool. (Use large apples).

CIDER BAKED APPLES

Use as many apples as you wish. Core carefully. Place in saucepan, upright, and add cider about half covering apples. Simmer and then boil gently until fruit is barely tender. Don't cover the fruit, but cover the pan. Save the cider and remove apples to serving dish.
Add to the cider 1 cup light brown sugar, the grated rind of 1 lemon. Simmer until reduced to about 1 cup. (You may have to adjust depending on number of apples used). Remove from heat, cool and pour over the apples.
Serve with roast or cold meat.

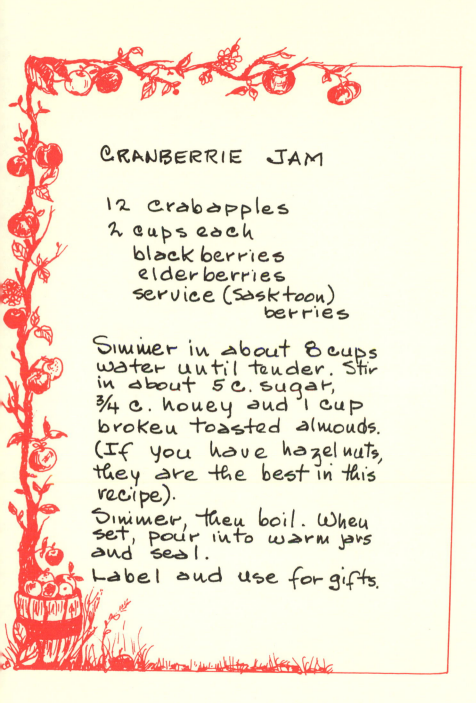

CRANBERRIE JAM

12 crabapples
2 cups each
    black berries
    elder berries
    service (sasktoon)
            berries

Simmer in about 8 cups
water until tender. Stir
in about 5 c. sugar,
3/4 c. honey and 1 cup
broken toasted almouds.
(If you have hazel nuts,
they are the best in this
recipe).
Simmer, then boil. When
set, pour into warm jars
and seal.
Label and use for gifts.

APPLE PIE with MOLASSES

There are various versions of a deep dish apple pie. I like this one, especially on a cold snowy night, served with hot spiced cider.

Pare and slice thin about 10 cups apples. (Usually 6 apples or 3 pounds)
3/4 cup light brown sugar
4 T. flour   — 1/2 tsp. cinnamon
1/4 tsp. each ground nutmeg and salt
1/2 cup light molasses
1/2 cup apple cider (I've used juice)
4 T. butter — heavy cream

Prepare pastry for 2 crusts to fit a 11 3/4 x 7 1/2 x 1 3/4 inch baking pan.

Combine apples with flour, sugar, spices and salt. Toss gently, then turn into bottom crust.

(Continued)

178

APPLE PIE with MOLASSES (Cont'd)

Combine molasses and apple cider and heat until it boils. Boil gently, uncovered, about 5 minutes. Stir in the butter, then pour mixture over the sliced apples.

Top baking dish with crust, cutting several slits to allow steam to escape. Fit securely over apples, pressing edges with fork tines.

Bake about 1 hour at 375°, or until apples are tender and the juices bubble over the top.

Serve warm with heavy (or light) cream poured over top.

179

Milk was a dangerous drink in the early days in No. America. Abraham Lincoln's mother died of "milk-silk". Cider was the popular drink – cheap and plentiful, and "hardened" into an alcoholic drink.

Nova Scotia's Annapolis Valley is well known for its apples; however, N.S. is a dwarf among the giant apple producing regions/countries. N.S. produces less than 2 o/o of the total North American production.

HOLIDAY CHUTNEY

Chop and combine:
1 quart each, apples and onions
1 cup each currants + sultana raisins
3 bananas, firm ones are better
Gently mix together, then add
1 cup wine vinegar.
1 cup broken slivered almonds
1 lb. light brown sugar
1/4 tsp. cayenne — dash of salt

Mix well. <u>Do not cook.</u> Let
stand, covered, about 1 hour.
Bottle, using pretty jars.

APPLE MARMALADE

Peel, core and thinly slice about
3 pounds tart apples. Add
about 1 heaping Tablespoon
butter to a heavy skillet.
Add the apples, 1 vanilla
bean, thinly pared rind of
1 large lemon and the juice.
Cover and cook slowly -
until apples are tender -
about 25 minutes.

Remove Vanilla bean and
lemon rind, then add about
1/4 cup sugar - or to taste,
and a heaping Teaspoon of
softened butter.

Cook over high heat, stir
constantly. When puree
is very thick, remove from
stove and cool.

This recipe can be used for
pie filling - with a lattice top!

Women were first admitted to the
N.S. Fruit Grower's Assoc. in 1884.
Susan Chase was the first female
President in 1928.

ORCHARD SNOW

Prepare about 6 small tart apples.
Lightly steam until soft enough to
mash. Sweeten with sugar and
vanilla to taste. Whisk 3 egg
whites until stiff and fold into
the apple mixture.

This dessert can be served with
your favourite topping. A thrifty
idea is to make a plain boiled
custard using the three egg yolks.
If time is a factor, try a quick
lemon sauce:
　　Boil about ¾ c. sugar with
¼ c. water. Remove and add
1 heaping T. of butter and the
juice of 1 small lemon. Mix well.

"Chyldren love an apple more
than golde." 1398

183

Nova Scotia Mincemeat

1½ qts. cooked chopped venison (beef)
4 qts. chopped apples - 2 qts. water
2½ qts. sugar - 1 qt. suet
2 cups water - ½ lb. chopped citron
1 - 11 oz. pkg. currants - 6 tsp. cinnamon
3 - 15 oz. pkgs. raisins - 3 tsp. mace
Grated rind + juice - 1 lemon, 2 oranges
2 tsp. gr. cloves - 1 tsp. nutmeg
4 tsp. vanilla extract
4 T. salt

Cook meat in water and save the liquid. Chop apples, meat and suet. Combine all ingredients in large canning kettle. Stir often until apples are tender. Seal in sterile jars.

Note:
In the early fall, when the apples are ripe and beginning to fall, try some prepared mock mincemeat with sliced pared tart apples - about 1 cup to a quart of mincemeat - or to taste - and a half cup rum or brandy.

184

WALLA WALLA CASSEROLE

4 cups each thinly sliced apples
  and thinly sliced sweet potatoes
2 tsp. instant minced onion
¾ cup each apple juice, maple syrup
½ cup melted butter
12 brown'n'serve pork sausages

Grease 2-quart casserole. Fill
with alternate layers of apple
and sweet potato, sprinkling each
layer with minced onion and salt.
Combine juice, syrup and butter,
pour over all. Cover. Bake at
350° for I hour. Place sausages
on top and bake, uncovered,
15 to 20 minutes longer or until
sausages are brown and
apples and potatoes are tender.

APPLE BUTTER:
A sauce made of
apples stewed
down in cider.
          1860

185

The apple -- a member of the Rose family -- is more widely grown than any other fruit.

BOSTON BLVD. SQUARES

Cream ⅔ c. butter with 2 c. brown sugar. Mix in 2 beaten eggs and 1 tsp. almond extract. Mix well.
Add:
2 c. flour   - 2 tsp. baking powder and a dash of salt. Stir well. Fold in 1 brimming cup chopped apples and ½ c. chopped nuts. Bake in buttered pan about 35 minutes at 350°. Cool on rack. Sprinkle powdered sugar over the top.

This recipe was a prize-winner in 1981 in Lansing, Michigan
"Anyway You Slice iT
Recipe Contest."

186

PENNSYLVANIA PIE

Line Dutch oven pan with dough. Cover bottom with a thick layer of sliced apples. Sprinkle with lemon juice (about 1 Tablespoon), 1 teaspoon cinnamon and ¼ cup soft butter. Top mixture with ½ cup molasses drizzled over the top. Add another layer of apples and top with another ½ cup molasses. Top with crust, brush lightly with milk and bake at 325° for 1½-2 hours.

"The first apple orchards in the New World were in Nova Scotia, New England, Pennsylvania, and the cider intake of the colonists... gargantuan proportions, and enjoyed by all members of the household."

187

IRENES APPLE BREAD

½ c. butter   —   ¾ cup sugar
2 eggs   —   1¾ c. sifted flour
1 tsp. baking powder - ½ tsp. salt
½ tsp. baking soda   — ¼ tsp. ginger
1 cup grated apples - ⅓ c. nutmeats
½ cup grated sharp cheddar
                              cheese

Cream butter until consistency
of mayonnaise, adding sugar
a little at a time. Add one
egg, beat; add second egg
and beat.
Combine flour, baking powder,
baking soda, salt and ginger
and add to first mixture, alt-
ernately with the apples. Stir
in the cheese and chopped
nuts.
Spoon into greased loaf pan
8x5x3 inches. Bake about 1 hour
at 350°.   Cool well, on rack,
before cutting.

188

GRANUILLE APPLE ROLL

Cream together ½ cup butter and
½ cup sugar. Add 2 egg yolks,
¼ cup milk and 2 cups flour
sifted with 2 teaspoons baking
powder. Knead well, then roll
out between 2 sheets wax paper
until ¼" thick.
Spread the dough with contents
1 can (15ozs) apple pie filling
mixed with 6 Tablespoons brown
sugar and grated rind of 1 lemon.
Dot with extra butter and roll as
you would a jelly roll. Place
in a buttered dish, slash at
regular intervals. Bake a half
hour at 350°. Serve warm—as
is or with cream.

189

APPLE PIE WITH A SNAP

Mix 1 ¾ cups of crushed ginger snaps with 8 Tablespoons melted butter. Press firmly into a 10" pie pan.

Beat 2 - 8 oz. packages cream cheese until smooth. Add 2 eggs and beat well.

Mix together ¼ cup of sugar, ¼ cup of flour, 1 cup apple-sauce and 2 Tablespoons lemon juice. Blend well with cheese mixture. Smooth into crust.

Bake about 1 hour at 350°. Cool. Just before serving, top with applesauce sprinkled with nutmeg.

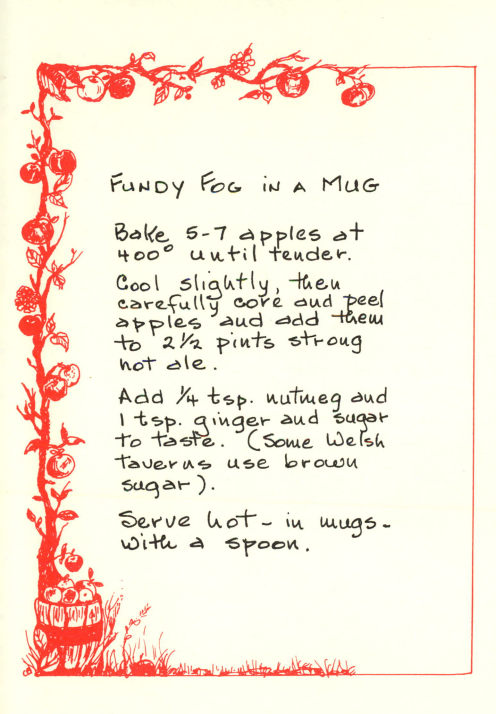

FUNDY FOG IN A MUG

Bake 5-7 apples at 400° until tender.

Cool slightly, then carefully core and peel apples and add them to 2½ pints strong hot ale.

Add ¼ tsp. nutmeg and 1 tsp. ginger and sugar to taste. (Some Welsh taverns use brown sugar).

Serve hot - in mugs - with a spoon.

CRABAPPLE - ROSEMARY JELLY

Rosemary is one of my favourite herbs and one that I use, fresh, year-round.

Chop enough crabapples to make 1 quart. Combine with 2 cups water and simmer until tender. Drain in jelly bag and measure the juice — to each cup add 1¾ - 2 cups sugar. Boil, swirling about 8-10 "leaves" of Rosemary in the liquid. Cool, skim and ladle into prepared glasses, but first try to find and remove the rosemary. Just before sealing, add 1 fresh rosemary leaf to each glass. Seal.

"Blossom Time" Bone China:

	1937	1985
Cup + Saucer -	$ .90 —	$ 21.95
dinner plate -	1.25 —	32.00
Tea pot (6 cup)	3.50 —	84.95

Apple-mose: a dish made with the pulp of stewed apples and other ingredients.

CANDIED APPLES with NUTS

Roll apples, with wooden skewers inserted, in chopped roasted peanuts after dipping in taffy. Here is one of many recipes:

2 cups sugar — 2/3 cups water
2 T. butter — 2 T. liquid glucose

Dissolve sugar in water and add butter and glucose. Cook until 300°. Stand in bowl of hot water so apples can be dipped easily. Coat each apple well and stand on wax paper.

The apple aided Newton in the discovery of gravity

193

APPLE AND ALMOND TART

PASTRY for 10" pie or tart pan.
Line the pan and flute edges,
then chill until firm. Heat
oven to 400°.

Almond cream
Cream about ½ cup butter,
gradually adding same amount
of sugar. Gently add 1 egg,
lightly beaten. When well
mixed, add 1 egg yolk and stir
well.
Add 2 teaspoons Kirsch, then
about ½ cups ground blanched
almonds and about ¼ cup flour.
Spread ⅔ of almond cream
over bottom of pastry shell.

Pare, core and slice apples-
very thin slices. Arrange
over almond cream, making
a wheel pattern. Press
lightly to flatten. Fill spaces
with remaining almond cream.
(Continued)

194

(Cont'd.)

Place baking sheet on bottom
rack. Set pie in centre and
bake about 15 minutes. Reduce
heat to 375° and bake 10
minutes more, or until apples
are tender.

Sprinkle pie with sugar and
bake another 20 minutes.
Cool on a rack.

Just before serving, top the
pie with brushed softened
apricot jam glaze.

This is an elegant recipe
from Normandy.

FRUIT STUFFING for PORK

Select number of pork steaks, cut ½" thick or as desired. Trim fat and split through center making a pocket.

Cut up apricots that have soaked over night and mix with diced peeled apples. Stuff the pork and secure with string. Quickly brown the steaks in butter to which 1 small clove of crushed garlic has been added. Add water to cover bottom of baking dish, or use apple juice or cider. Cover. Cook at 350° for an hour or until pork is tender.

NEW YORK STATE is:

Second in the USA in both apple and cherry production –
First in applesauce
Second in apple juice
Second in canned and frozen apples

Goose Stuffing ②

Prepare about 5 apples and chop. This amount will vary according to size of the goose. Toss apples in about ¼ cup light brown sugar. Mix into apples and sugar, 1 pound of prunes that have been soaked all night and chopped.
Stuff the goose and baste it about 6-8 times with sweet cider.

Nova Scotia Paté

2 large apples, cooked with skins, pureed.
2 fillets smoked kippers, deboned, skinned.
Soften 8 ozs cream cheese with a large dill pickle finely chopped.
Combine pieces of kippers with cheese, apple pureé and juice of 1 lemon. Blend well and then chill well.
Serve with melba toast.

The probable origin of the apple -
south of the Caucasus from the
Caspian Sea to Trebizond on the
Black Sea. It spread westward
from Persia to the Atlantic and
through Europe thence northward
to Russia and westward to America.

APPLE CATSUP

Pare, core and chop 12 Apples.
Place in saucepan, cover with water,
simmer until soft and water almost
evaporated. Puree, and to each
quart add the following:

    1 cup sugar — 2 grated onions
    1 tsp. each mustard, cloves, cinnamon
    1 Tablespoon salt - 2 cups cider vinegar

Simmer gently one hour. Seal in
sterilized jars.

At the beginning of the Christian
era the Romans cultivated a few
varieties of Apples for eating raw.

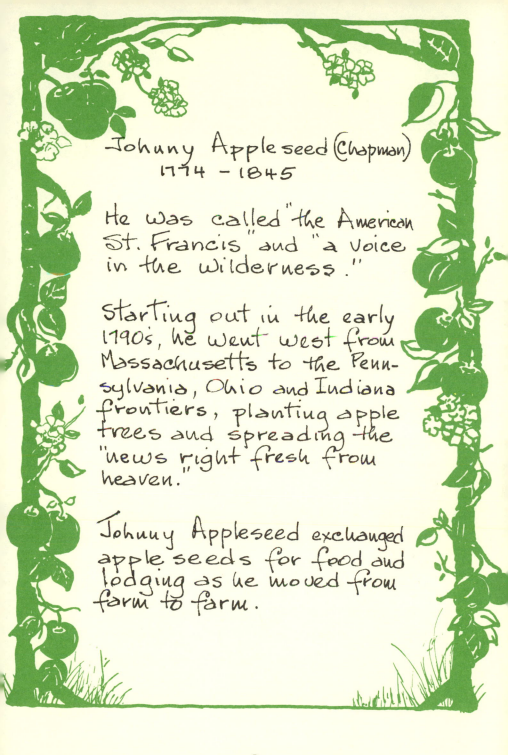

Johnny Apple seed (Chapman)
1774 – 1845

He was called "the American
St. Francis" and "a voice
in the wilderness."

Starting out in the early
1790's, he went west from
Massachusetts to the Pennsylvania, Ohio and Indiana
frontiers, planting apple
trees and spreading the
"news right fresh from
heaven."

Johnny Appleseed exchanged
apple seeds for food and
lodging as he moved from
farm to farm.

199

Historically, apples have had their ups and downs. In the Garden of Eden, they caused Adam a bushel of trouble.

GINGER-APPLE CUSTARD

3 lbs. apples - sliced
5 c. white bread chunks
2 c. buttermilk - 2 c. milk
1/2 c. molasses - 1/4 c. water
1/3 c. sugar - 4 eggs, lightly beaten
3/4 tsp. each nutmeg and ginger
1 tsp. cinnamon - 1/8 tsp. cloves
1/8 tsp black pepper - 1/4 tsp. salt

Let bread soak in buttermilk. Mix apples and water in a covered skillet and simmer but stop before apples get soft. Cool. Add rest of ingredients to bread mixture and fold in apples. Heap into greased casserole and bake about 1 hour at 350°. Serve warm.

APPLES AND RAISINS
(baked in a pie)

4 cups sliced apples
½ cup seedless raisins
2 T. frozen orange juice <u>concentrate</u>
½ tsp. cinnamon — 2 T. flour
¾ cup sugar — 3 T. butter

Combine sugar, flour, spice and a dash of salt. Mix with apples and raisins. Heap into unbaked crust. Sprinkle with orange juice and butter. Top with crust and bake 15 minutes at 400° and 40 minutes at 350°.

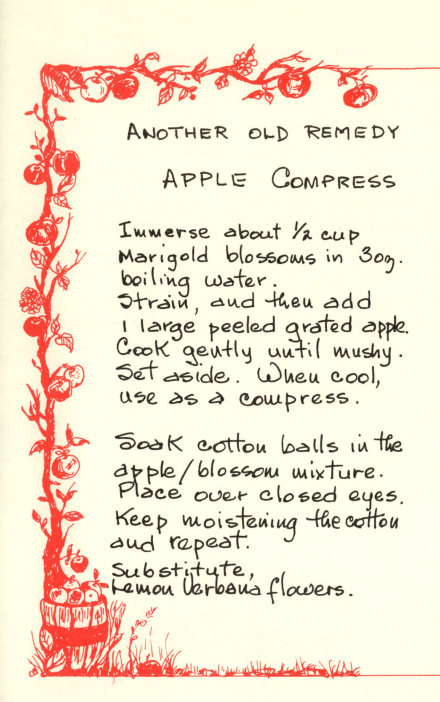

ANOTHER OLD REMEDY

APPLE COMPRESS

Immerse about ½ cup
Marigold blossoms in 3oz.
boiling water.
Strain, and then add
1 large peeled grated apple.
Cook gently until mushy.
Set aside. When cool,
use as a compress.

Soak cotton balls in the
apple/blossom mixture.
Place over closed eyes.
Keep moistening the cotton
and repeat.
Substitute,
Lemon Verbena flowers.

"The variation between the day and night temperatures in New Jersey, Delaware and the eastern part of Maryland and Virginia is about the same as that along the shores of Lake Ontario. In both instances we find fruit regions of the highest rank. The Annapolis Valley in Nova Scotia, alongside the Bay of Fundy, the east shore of Lake Michigan and the Pacific coast States are all fruit regions because of their climate."

Fraser 1924

OVEN APPLESAUCE

Place 4 large sliced cooking apples in a casserole dish. Mix 1/4 cup sugar, a dab of salt and 4 cloves and add to apples. Cover and bake a half hour at 350°. Cool slightly, remove cloves and gently mix in 3 Tablespoons butter in small pieces. Serve with roast.

GOOSE APPLE JAM

3 Tart cooking apples
1¼ lbs. gooseberries
3 cups sugar — Juice of 1 lemon

Clean up gooseberries and mash.
Sprinkle with 1½ cups sugar, mix
well and stand aside 24 hours.
Chop the apples and mix into
the berries. Boil gently, add
rest of the sugar and citrus
juice. Boil rapidly until jam is
ready to set.
Ladle into warm dry jars.
Variation: Include shredded
lemon rind with juice.

204

Kitchen at Cranberrie Cottage

205

SUCH SWEET CONNECTIONS!

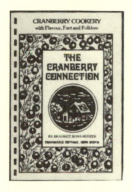

Each book $11.95
Available in stores everywhere

Published by **Nimbus Publishing Limited**
P.O. Box 9301
Station A
Halifax, N.S. B3K 5N5 Tel: (902) 454-8381